Coping with Family Stress

Dr Peter Cheevers is an award-winning playwright and author and has written an acclaimed television play. His writing includes published poetry, opinion pieces for magazines and newspapers, and *Coping with Seasonal Affective Disorder* (co-author Fiona Marshall, Sheldon Press, London, 2002).

Overcoming Common Problems Series

Selected titles

A full list of titles is available from Sheldon Press,
36 Causton Street, London SW1P 4ST and on our website at
www.sheldonpress.co.uk

Overcoming Common Problems Series

Overcoming Common Problems Series

Overcoming Common Problems

Coping with Family Stress
How to deal with difficult relatives

DR PETER CHEEVERS

First published in Great Britain in 2007

Sheldon Press
36 Causton Street
London SW1P 4ST

British Library Cataloguing-in-Publication Data
A catalogue record for this book is available from the British Library

ISBN 978-1-84709-018-8

1 3 5 7 9 10 8 6 4 2

Typeset by Fakenham Photosetting Ltd, Fakenham, Norfolk
Printed in Great Britain by Ashford Colour Press

Produced on paper from sustainable forests

Contents

Acknowledgements

I am very grateful to all those individual members of families who were trusting and open enough to share their experiences of stress in their family unit. They have provided an enormously useful aid to writing this book. I hope their honesty helps others. Of course they will not agree with everything I have said, so they are exonerated from any of my views put forward in the book. I am also indebted to previous thinkers and writers on the subject, too numerous to mention, who have written on, commented on, heaped praise on and cursed that thing we must all belong to, willingly or not – the family.

Note: This is not a medical book and is not intended to replace advice from your doctor. Do consult your doctor if you are feeling symptoms of stress with which you feel you need help.

Introduction

In the chimpanzee family, which is the species most like our own, prolonged grudge-bearing or lasting resentment after being hurt or even badly injured seems non-existent. Jane Goodall (in her book *In the Shadow of Man*) notes with interest how in chimps the usual effect of an injury results in a profoundly touching approach to the aggressor with a demand for reconciliation. What seems to be most noticed, Goodall observed, is not the injury itself, but the failure of the social bond. This is illustrated when the aggrieved or hurt chimp, after being threatened or attacked by a family superior, follows the aggressor, screaming and crouching low in apprehension. When close enough, the hurt party will hold out his hand to beg for a reassuring touch from the aggressor. The aggrieved chimp will not quieten or relax till he has been patted again and again on his head by his aggressor, or until given the final reassurance of the aggressor by his leaning forward to press his lips on his brow. In watching such family reconciliations, I defy anybody not to be moved and maybe, as I did, to feel a lump in the throat.

As Goodall points out, this reconciliation process makes it possible for members of the chimp family to resume the relationship as though the injury had never taken place. Without this natural sociability, the family unit would break down. Goodall also observes that in small children there is likewise a reconciliation process and a refusal to bear grudges for hurts. Yet when we come to the family of adult human beings, with their much stronger powers of memory, imagination and foresight, this simple reaction sometimes becomes impossible. No one wants to be someone who holds a grudge, but for many of us bearing a grudge against other members of the family is a major cause of stress. The irritating parent who still treats you as though you're 11, the abrasive and insensitive sister, the brother who never listens to you, the obnoxious uncle who can be guaranteed to spoil any family gathering – though we might like to deny it, they have the power to exasperate or infuriate us like nobody else. Yet the family is the strongest and most enduring influence in any person's life. That is why this book is concerned with how this unique influence may cause stress in members of families who are adults or near adulthood.

Family stress itself has been defined in different ways. Family stress expert Dr Pauline Boss, professor emeritus at the University of

Minnesota, has defined family stress as a pressure or tension in the family system. Another family stress researcher, Hamilton McCubbin, at the University of Wisconsin, defines family stress as an imbalance between the demands facing a family and the ability of that family to handle these demands.

However, rather than the notion of a family under stressful siege, in this book I am referring more to the kind of stress we may all experience from the dynamics of being an adult within a wider family unit. This may mean coping with other adults within the family system who are disruptive and dysfunctional, and who cause stress by their behaviour; or the stress could be because of an inherently difficult situation, such as illness. For some people too, stress doesn't have to involve a crisis, or unusual events, but can result from the ongoing pressure of everyday activities. The impact of ordinary external or internal stresses on families, not just key events, often spirals into damaging behaviour, both for the individual and for the larger family unit.

Adult sibling rivalry, coping with ageing parents, dealing with a family business, and ordinary family socializing, are just some of the themes that fall under this banner. Statements like 'My family's different', 'I've always been like that; I come from a difficult family', 'In this house, we always ...', 'In this house, you can never ...' are just some of the tell-tale sentences that pinpoint the kind of family stress I mean. For example, the words 'always' and 'never' can be real giveaways because they tend to indicate the pressure of entrenched behavioural patterns.

When people are of a so-called 'responsible' age, we expect them to be able to deal with such family influence. Surely they should be able to cope with the stress of family relationships in a mature and considered way? Unfortunately, that is not the reality. And, if left unchecked, this kind of family stress can damage beyond repair the workings of a family, and also the individuals in that family. The good news, though, is that there are many ways to strengthen both the individuals, and the families of which they are part, before the stress cracks appear.

Despite the fact that stress itself is one of the most common human experiences, it is surprisingly difficult to define. Hans Selye, an endocrinologist (endocrinology is the study of the glands and hormones) who popularized the notion of stress, said, 'Stress as a scientific concept suffers the misfortune of being too widely known and too poorly understood.' What we *can* say, though, is that stress, both to individuals or a whole family, is a force or event that affects normal stability, balance or functioning.

Stress involves change, and families are always changing. Babies become toddlers, older children become teenagers, parents return to work, grandparents age and grow frail. Children move schools, families move house, adults change jobs. There can be loss too: we lose jobs, significant others, homes. Anything that can change some aspect of the family system can produce stress.

Such changes in the family system are sometimes known as stressor events. They may not be bad in themselves; instead, it is how we perceive and interpret these events, as individuals and families, that causes the stress.

We are all members of families, but we are also individuals. A major way in which we view ourselves as individuals has been derived from what is called the 'social-atomistic' model. This was put forward by the English philosopher Thomas Hobbes (1588–1679) and argues that human beings are essentially separate individuals in a state of competition. This notion seems to have been built into the structure of capitalism. Perhaps it should have been consigned to the waste paper basket!

Fortunately, this model is not quite the whole truth. The reality is more that, like other primates, we humans are actually quite sociable and affectionate much of the time. However, if stressed, many of us can bear grudges against people – and that of course includes other family members.

The study of animal behaviour (ethology) concerning stress is a telling mirror to our own behaviour, and on the issue of bearing grudges, we might have something to learn from the chimpanzee – which, as we've already said, is the species most like our own.

As I hope to show in this book, how we actually *perceive* stress is the key to a healthier and happier life. This doesn't involve a revolutionary change, nor is it a battle plan where we blitzkrieg those who don't agree with us. It is in fact nothing more than learning how to change our perceptions of family stressors, both gradually and by using practical methods. As Albert Einstein once said concerning looking at things in a different way: 'It is not about demolishing the old hut and erecting a shining new skyscraper in its place. It is rather like steadily climbing a mountain and gaining new and wider views as we do so.'

I hope that by the end of this book you will be able to recognize why stress occurs in the family; what the danger signals are; what this stress does to people; and how it affects the larger family unit if allowed to spread unchecked. Most importantly, I hope the book will provide coping mechanisms for the individuals in the family, so they are no longer passive sufferers of family stress.

The book is organized in the following way. Chapter 1 is an overview of how our modern-day family has been formed, while Chapter 2 looks at what forms stress in the family might take. Chapter 3 examines 'family myths' and how these affect our view of who we are. Perception, a key factor in managing family stress, is the theme of Chapter 4.

We then turn to specifics. Chapter 5 spans the stress pitfalls and remedies of the family business, and Chapter 6 is a brief look at the strains and stress on the family carer. Chapter 7 covers family deaths, wills and funerals, and Chapter 8 looks at those flashpoint situations with which we may be all too familiar – such as Christmas and holidays.

In Chapter 9 there are practical suggestions for improving family relationships; Chapter 10 deals with another key factor in managing family stress: how good your social support system is. Chapter 11 looks at cognitive behavioural therapy and also examines ways in which you might explore and re-define your family. Finally, Chapter 12 explores several coping mechanisms including diet, exercise, relaxation and various therapies.

1

The family

Not so long ago, in the overall span of the 4,600,000,000 or so years ago that our planet Earth was formed, nomadic tribes embraced uncertainty. No doubt these wanderers had their own forms of culture, politics, religion and social mores, but today we are more likely to seek out certainty, and to look at the values of former generations with bewilderment. But however different we may think we are today, the past values of our forebears are embroidered into our DNA and laced into the fabric of our thinking. So, when understanding the stress process today, we need to recognize that stress occurs in a unique socio-historical context which affects how we behave both as individuals and families.

The family's response then is influenced by the particular historical period in which it lives; its cultural identity; the economic conditions of society; the family's genetic stamina and resistance; and the stages in the family life cycle. As is pointed out in the volume *A History of the Family* (André Burguière et al., eds, Harvard University Press 1996), the family in one form or another is at the heart of every society. It is as old as the prehistoric bones jumbled in caves, and as new as the latest union consummated in a test tube. It is our most common institution, and it is also the source of some of the world's most compelling and persistent questions, touching the very quick of history, anthropology, psychology and sociology.

'Honour your father and mother'

Biblical history, for instance, is largely family history. 'Honour your father and mother' says the fourth commandment. Stories in the Bible give graphic warning of the danger of family disunity. The story of Cain and Abel is salutary precisely because it involves the violent killing of one's own brother. Such stories remind us how important it is that family members love and respect one another. When these qualities are lacking, the family becomes dysfunctional; in other words, it fails in its 'God intended' purpose. When family ties are violated, all relationships become strained. Many biblical stories strike at the very foundation of society – the family.

The belief still holds strong that the family unit is the building block for all societies, perhaps along with the assumption that family relationships are the epitome for all other social relations. The family is that rock, the pillar of society, that fundamental cell in the national organism and society's shock-absorber of social change. After all, you wouldn't expect a person to do more for a stranger or an acquaintance than that person would do for a family member. And if the family breaks down, it cannot – like Humpty Dumpy – be put back together again. And this, of course, has grave consequences for society.

Originally 'family' meant a band of slaves

The Latin equivalent of the word family, *familiola*, meant in classical times a small band of slaves, a meaning that continued even after it extended to people affiliated by blood and marriage. For many centuries, however, the notion of family referred to authority relations rather than loved ones.

The sentimentalization of family life came about with the emergence of competitive individualism, when more and more people started seeking to attain the 'good things' of life. This was a pursuit fostered by the economic system we call capitalism. Stephanie Coontz, in *The Way We Never Were*, argues that with the emergence of capitalism it was useful (functional) to sentimentalize the family.

Influences on families across the globe

Throughout the centuries and across the globe, families have been re-defined by seismic events: from the Spanish conquest of that vast tract of central Mexico to northern Honduras; to India, where the effects of British colonial policy and nationalistic reform impacted on the family; to the spread of Islam in new family codes in black Africa; to today's '4, 2, 1' phenomenon in China, where government policies have long dictated that there should be only one child per family so that today you have the phenomenon of one child growing up and being expected to support two parents and four grandparents.

However, when we talk of the Western family unit (which includes those countries whose dominant views are derived from European culture) we can see that the forms and norms of the Western family unit have been shaped by the shock of 'modernity'. There are varying views of what 'modernity' actually is. For many it refers to a period extending from the late sixteenth and early seventeenth centuries (in the case of Europe) to the mid to late twentieth century. It is often associated with capitalism and the quality of being 'current' or 'of the present': 'a shopping mall would instil a spirit of modernity into this village' is one way of looking at it. The idea of 'progress' – that life gets progressively better – is an assumption that might be said to serve as modernism's backbone.

Other factors that have influenced the family

How the Industrial Revolution shaped the family

The Industrial Revolution brought increased travel and mobility, which vastly widened people's social horizons and opportunities. Travel by train multiplied the number of potential encounters between men and women. For the first time in many centuries, women were able to judge and compare their male partners to others. Increasingly, women chose to opt out of relationships that they considered to be dysfunctional or inadequate. Today, over three-quarters of all divorces in the West are initiated by women.

The Sixties and freedom for women

Wars and economic upheavals followed the Industrial Revolution and led to the forced introduction of women into the labour market, leading to an increase in economic opportunities. In the 1960s came the contraceptive pill and safer sex. In the face of this newfound freedom and the realities of changing sexual conduct, the double moral standard crumbled. Social and ethical codes changed for women. The resulting sexual revolution affected both sexes, but the main beneficiaries were women whose sexuality was suddenly legitimized. No longer living under the cloud of unwanted pregnancies, women became aware of their needs, priorities, preferences, wishes and, in general, of their proper emotions. They cast off thought patterns inculcated in them by patriarchal societies. Women's growing control over their bodies – which had been objectified, reviled and admired for millennia by men – is arguably one of the most striking features of the feminine revolution.

The effect of technology on the family

More recently, technology has evolved, scattering our sources of information. Instead of information being in one place, as in Victorian times when the source of information was the pulpit on Sunday morning, now we live with a myriad of informational sources which pursues us relentlessly. The media loudhailers are never turned off. They are always addressing us, advising us, cajoling us, tempting us. Advertisers inculcate desire in us, and desire can only be quenched by buying things. Added to this are the faxes, mobiles, iPods, the internet, e-mail – what we often refer to as 'informational overload' or 'meltdown'.

In fact, many stress counsellors advise that periodically turning the whole 'circus' off – no phones, no television, no technology – can be a very effective anti-stress therapy.

The legal redistribution of wealth from men to women

Over time, the legal system has shifted to allow men and women to jointly own marital property, and the result of this has been a major (and ongoing) redistribution of wealth from men to women. Add to this the disparities in life expectancy between the two genders (women live longer than men) and the significance of the transfer of economic resources becomes clear.

As a result of all these advances in women's rights, in some legal respects the bias is now against men, although persistent imbalances in salaries, and the lower numbers of women in board rooms or Parliament, is still very evident.

Single-parent families

Added to such seismic social changes, the family itself has changed dramatically, as is clearly evident today in the social acceptance of the non-nuclear and single-parent family. One-third of all children in developed countries now grow up in single-parent families.

Although economically disadvantaged, most single-parent families are presently headed by women. Today, one-third of all children in developed countries grow up in single-parent families with no male figure around to serve as a role model. Many people choose to live together rather than marry, and over a quarter of all children in the UK are born to unmarried cohabiting parents.

The changing family

The Greek philosopher Heraclitus said, 'All is flux. You cannot step into the same river twice.' And so it has been for the family: change, or stress, seems ever constant.

Yet at the end of this analysis of the changing family, the point is that the family persists and is still revered. This reverence gives impetus to a range of patterns of behaviour and values, including loyalty, personal contributions ('I'm doing this for my family') and sacrifices ('I am prepared to go without if it helps my family').

Looking back at the family through history, then, the evidence suggests that what we call 'the family' is itself a historical construct, ideologically assembled. This means that we view the family through cultural spectacles, lenses that we should maybe become aware of if we are to understand the family stress we encounter and how we are primed to react to it.

The imaginary family?

For Donald Lowe, the concept of 'the family' is a highly important and useful 'imaginary'. But what does this mean, and what are the influences that would make our concepts of the family an 'imaginary'? Let's take just one, advertising.

'Late capitalism' is a term sometimes used to refer to the capitalism of the second half of the twentieth century. Advertising, depending on your point of view, might be said to be 'the jewel in the crown' or the 'spear in the side' of late capitalism. In advertising, the image of the family is used to sell everything from 'home-cooked' frozen dinners to political candidates. The job of advertisers is to inculcate desire. However, it is well to be aware that people have power over you only if they have something that they think you need.

Through advertising, we are urged to find happiness outside of ourselves by getting more, buying more, doing more. Which brings us to the modern-day phenomenon of 'shopping'. Jean-Jacques Rousseau, the eighteenth-century philosopher, wrote, 'Man is born free and is everywhere in chains.' More recent commentators refer to us 'being everywhere in chain stores'! The image of the family is used in commercials to sell products on the basis that the 'traditional' family is the 'happy' family. As a result, an image of the 'family' is represented to us, and we in turn use this imagery to represent a notion of 'family' that we should live by.

Families that advertisers would have us live by

In many commercials the representation of 'the family' is frequently coded by the use of the 'mother' figure, often used to signify nurturing care, or domestic duty, or both, and by locating the mother in the household environment it explicitly suggests care for one's own children. So, a product will be seen as necessary for 'care and duty'. Whether it's soup on a winter's day, or pet food on a spring day, wallpaper or the latest family car, it becomes imbued with the ideology associated with the mother, and is seen as necessary for the 'happy' family.

In these 'happy family' commercials, the general message is that the family works because both males and females are involved, with 'action' coming from the males (say, football) and 'nurturing' from the females (resolving a problem). For instance, the mother may act as peacemaker when the older males will not allow the younger male to play, and we are shown that it takes the female intervention to resolve the issue. According to professor of sociology Gayle Kaufman, who carried out a 1999 study entitled 'The Portrayal of Men's Family Roles in Television Commercials', fathers play a largely passive role. In the few instances where the male does take an active role – such as a household chore – his assistance is 'shown to be incompetent' or the wife 'must guide him through the chore'. The father is depicted as being adorably ineffectual, and this incompetence is shown to be necessary to the family.

The mass appeal of this 'reinforcer' type of commercial relies on viewers believing the ideal of male and female figureheads (the nuclear family consisting of two married, heterosexual parents and their legal children) as the only appropriate way to raise a child. Through the media, we are subject to this sort of imagery and it affects our thinking about the family we live in, and how that family should behave. Such advertising presents templates of families we should live by.

'Should' is the word, however. Today, men and women might look to the family for economic and social support, but if the family fails as an economic and social launching pad, people may lose interest and begin looking for alternatives. This trend of disintegration has been further enhanced by technological innovation which has encouraged self-sufficiency and unprecedented social segmentation that has resulted in the breaking up of many families.

Despite the conservative appeal of this kind of advertising, then, it is probably true that today the nuclear family is often a ramshackle version of this image. Yet every family, whether nuclear, single-parent, same-gender or extended, does have a structure, whether dysfunctional or functional, chaotic or rigid.

Real families and mythical families

John Gillis, a professor of history at Rutgers University, has studied the way that we have real, physical families, and also mythical or imaginary families – both of which have a tremendous influence on us. We can divide this into 'families we live with', and 'families we live by'.

'Families we live with' are the people with whom we quarrel over access to the bathroom on a daily basis – families as defined by the census and social survey research. In other words, co-resident members of households who define themselves as related to one another. 'What is the number of your house, and what is the postal district?' The computer screen will tell the operative at the other end of the phone that there is a family living at 33 Acacia Avenue with two adults and three children.

However, the 'families we live by' will not be found in census tables or statistical surveys. 'Families we live by' not only occupy a much larger space than the household, but are extended over time, belonging to the past and the future as much as to the present. They are mental constructs – or myths – that include a far more extended array of kin, including both the dead and the unborn. You will probably be familiar with family phrases such as: 'You are a frustrated preacher, just like your great-grandfather', 'That anger comes from your grandmother's side', 'Your Uncle Albert was the one. He was your uncle on your mother's side, if he had lived ... how things would have been different. He was the powerhouse of the family', 'You see, it runs in the family' (bad temper, genius, being late).

The 'families we live by' are no less real to us than the people we live with on a day-to-day basis. They are made real, according to Gillis, through a set of cultural practices or rituals that are so embedded in our contemporary culture that they largely go unrecognized and unquestioned. Family photographs, family holidays, and events such as weddings, are among the rituals we take for granted. These assumptions and rituals don't spring from nowhere – they have a context and a history.

To challenge and expand our notions of family, it may be useful to look at the list of subjects researched by Gillis's students, including:

- Homes within the family home: bedrooms, basements, dens
- Homes away from the family home: dorms, second homes, camps
- 'Haunted' family houses
- Family cars, pets, meals
- The 'black sheep' of the family
- Family rites of passage (teenagers)
- Alternative families
- Sibling relations
- Family holidays, families' seasonal get-togethers
- Family heirlooms
- Family gift giving
- Family weddings and funerals.

Not all of the above may ring any bells, but, as an exercise, go through the list and write brief notes on the topics that leap out at you. Questions to consider might be:

- Did you have an 'alternative family' as a teenager in the form of friends? Perhaps you still have one now? Who are your main sources of emotional support – friends or family?
- Did or does your family home have a 'character' of its own? Is it 'haunted' by certain family themes and characteristics? For example, 'This house is impossible to keep tidy', 'Why don't you just hang up the car keys where they are meant to hang, honestly!', 'It's hard for us to have people round because this house is so disorganized'.
- When a significant family member died, did you 'inherit'? That is, was your relationship acknowledged by means of an heirloom or a token of remembrance from the deceased? Or did it all go to family members who were 'closer'? If you did 'inherit', are you happy with the family identity bestowed upon you?

2

What constitutes family stress?

'Family' is among the three leading sources of stress, according to a classic 1967 (updated in 2006) study by Thomas H. Holmes and Richard H. Rahe, from the University of Washington. Likewise, according to the Samaritans' 'Stressed Out' Survey, the family is the second biggest cause of stress, with one in five Britons experiencing problems at home. Significantly, research shows that family stresses affect women three times as much as men.

Research by psychologist Dr Leonard Felder, family therapist and author of *When Difficult Relatives Happen to Good People*, found that over 70 per cent of us have a frustrating or difficult relative. In one survey of women aged between 20 and 45, 45 per cent confessed to taking out the stress in their daily lives on those closest to them, shouting at family members or resorting to eating junk food for comfort when faced with the stress and strains of family.

The survey revealed some other worrying habits, with 41 per cent saying that stress led to them losing sleep. In the 20–24 age group, almost a quarter admitted to getting drunk regularly, though on the plus side, this group was also most likely to go to the gym. Depression can often be a consequence of long-term stress. Chronic family stress is also associated with increased illness in children, according to a study by a team at the University of Rochester.

The good news is that this stress is not set in stone, as I hope you'll see if you read on.

So just what is family stress?

According to a report in the *New York Times*, the Navajo Nation Council protested that the hanta virus, which killed 40 people in the early 1990s, including many Navajo Indians, should not be named after a canyon on its reservation. The council voted 52 to 0 on Thursday to ask the Centers for Disease Control and Prevention not to recommend naming the virus 'Muerto Canyon Hantavirus'. The Federal Centers proposed the name recently, saying it was following a custom of naming diseases after the place where they were discovered.

This little tale of the Navajo Indians' robust reaction to a naming process is relevant. For words cause us to react, so it is of interest how such a word as 'stress' came about. Our behaviour around something is influenced by its name.

The word 'stress' is of Latin origin, from *strictus*, past participle of *stringere*, 'to draw tight', and has been a part of the English language since at least the fourteenth century. Its earliest meaning, in Middle English (*stresse*), was 'hardship', and the word came partly from *destresse* ('distress'), from Old French, and partly from Old French *estrece*, meaning 'narrowness' or 'oppression'. Other early meanings included several definitions such as 'adversity' and 'affliction'. Over the centuries the use of the term continued to be broadened. Today the *Oxford English Dictionary* (1989, p. 885) defines stress as 'strain upon a bodily organ or mental power'.

Out of all these, perhaps my own personal favourite definition of stress with regard to the family is the first one – that unique feeling of being constricted and constrained that the family seems able to produce like nothing else.

Is your family a source of stress?

How many of the following ring a bell?

- Do you avoid specific family members who you know will criticize you or give you harsh advice?
- Do you spend time during the day thinking resentfully of a family member, or arguing in your head with him or her?
- Do you find you're incoherent with rage, or lost for words, when you try to describe some members of your family?
- Do you communicate by e-mail or letter and avoid meetings and the phone because you know from bitter experience that verbal communication just doesn't work?
- Do you have a family member who is rude or insulting to your own children or partner?
- Is there an ongoing money argument in your family – for example, as a result of a will?
- Do you feel invisible at family gatherings?
- Is there a family member who makes you cringe with his or her comments about race, gender, sexuality or spirituality?
- Does your family use sarcasm and 'humour' to put down you or other family members?
- Do you have conflict over a family business?

- Do you dread opening e-mails or letters from some family members?
- Do you feel you routinely give, while your difficult family member is one of life's takers?
- Do you dread the obligatory family gathering at Christmas or other family occasions, or find it stressful to tell members of your family that you don't want to attend?
- Do you suffer stress symptoms as a result of contact with your family: irritability, feeling faint, drained or exhausted?
- Do you ever wish your family was more like other people's – less difficult, less weird, more normal, more supportive?

Denial is the most common response to family stress and frustrations, according to Dr Leonard Felder. But it is important to recognize stress situations and to take action, because stress, especially ongoing stress, has an important impact on the body.

Hillary

The ground seemed ridiculously far away. As her brain's amygdale (linked to the brain's fear and pleasure response) recognized danger, her heart began to beat up to three times faster; her blood pressure increased; her mouth became uncomfortably dry because the parasympathetic (not under conscious control) nervous system was inhibited and had stopped producing saliva. The perception of the risk she was taking had sent her system into top gear, producing a massive surge of adrenaline, noradrenaline and growth hormone. She was breathing much faster now and blood surged around her body, into her muscles. Her pupils dilated, allowing her to perceive movement around her more clearly, and to see into the shadows and darkness which might have concealed further threat. Her immune system geared up to deal with any potential injuries.

But Hillary, on her first parachute jump for charity, landed safely, and thought the experience exhilarating, although her family got very 'stressed out' about it all.

The vast majority of us will never subject ourselves to that degree of stress. We might, however, suffer surprisingly similar symptoms when facing a family problem.

Martin

Each day, as Martin goes to his teaching job, he must drive across a suspension bridge over a major river.

Martin's head is full of the family; he's just had yet another row with his brother, his mother is more interested in her weekly Lottery ticket than the fact that he's just completed his second degree; his teenage daughter was late again coming home last night; he wasn't invited to his great-aunt's funeral, and a visiting uncle from Ireland has snubbed him.

Just as another gust of wind buffets the bridge, Martin's agitation about his family continues to fan the bushfire that is his stress. Martin is not about to call on any coping skills to deal with this stress over his family because he cannot specify what is causing it.

However, if Martin cared to check, I'm sure he would agree that his behaviour around his family is frequently manifesting some of the following:

- Guilt
- Bickering
- Explosive arguments
- Sense of frustration
- Little time to spend together
- Conversations centred on time and tasks, rather than people and feelings
- Constant rushing from place to place
- Escaping into work or other activities.

Martin will also face, as we all do, some of the more serious stress events for families:

- Bereavement
- Illness or injury
- Divorce
- Moving house
- Children leaving home
- Job change
- Arguments with a spouse or other family member
- Difficulties with children's behaviour or with their educational performance.

Such a list of life events makes it obvious that a certain amount of family stress is inevitable for all of us.

Disturbance of the family's steady state can of course be desirable at times; life transitions are essential for psychological development. It is *how* a family handles and copes with stress that is truly important. Just because family stress is universal doesn't mean we don't need to find out what causes our particular family conflict.

Understanding stress

Martin again

Martin is being urged by a colleague at work to ask himself questions as to why he is always feeling so stressed.

One day Martin gets to the suspension bridge and sees a sign that it has been closed for repairs. The bridge, he finds out later from this colleague, is stressed. This stress is caused by an imbalance between the force of the winds and the strength of the structure.

Martin's colleague explains, 'The stress of a strong wind might alter the balance of a suspension bridge so that the bridge imperceptibly swings from side to side. Suppose the bridge could be likened to us. Just as we are buffeted by events in our everyday lives, if we don't deal with them by slowing down, then some of us have to close down for repairs.'

This colleague delivers this with a jocular air that disguises his concern, for he sometimes worries about the rather intense Martin, who is always going on about his family.

Like many other people, Martin has not given 'stress' much serious thought. But to understand the wider term 'family stress', we need to understand the general stress that undergirds it.

Stress interacts with our nervous system. There are two branches of the nervous system. The voluntary system controls conscious movement, whereas the autonomic nervous system (ANS) controls involuntary and automatic bodily activity. It is the latter that is involved in the stress response.

However, the causes of stress can still remain unclear, for the things that cause stress for you may not be a problem for your neighbour, and things that bring stress to your neighbour's life may not worry you at all. This is why stress is difficult for scientists to define, especially as it has become commonly used to cover a whole spectrum of emotions and feelings. There are many varying classifications of stress. Some researchers distinguish between 'Eustress', when something changes for the better, and 'Distress', when something changes for the worse. Others use 'stress' to cover anxiety: the fear of what *may* happen.

Good stress, bad stress

Because stress can enhance our immediate ability to cope – say, preparing to make that speech at a family wedding – it can be considered 'good' stress, being a 'short-term stressor'. Likewise, watching your daughter in the school play may be stressful, but because it is short term it can be termed 'good' stress. However, if stress persists, then it may well be classed as 'bad' stress. Long-term stressful situations – say a family conflict, separation or divorce; the tug of war in loyalties towards a parent's new spouse; discord among siblings due to the pressures of caring for an ageing parent – these can all cause long-term stress to individuals.

In such situations, the nervous system remains activated and continues to pump out extra stress hormones. Over an extended period, this can wear out the body's reserves, leaving a person feeling depleted, and weakening the body's immune system. If the stress is not dealt with, eventually it may lead to behaviour that appears to resolve the issue, but in fact merely avoids it – for example, anxiety (escape) or depression (withdrawal). One very common mode of escape is binge eating. Numerous studies have shown that stress is the major cause of binge eating. Binge eating is a perfect example of how not to react to stress because such short-term escapes lead to long-term imprisonment.

'Stress' is the new shorthand for 'I'm really busy'

People sport the badge of the cultural values of their decade. The 1960s were laid back, 'Hey, far out, man'. In the 1980s, it was about materialism, boasting about possessions. But crowing the praises of the new car you've acquired, or being 'out of it' as in the Sixties, are not the best social entrées today.

However, being really busy and having an important job are. Stress comes with this territory, and for many it has become the new status symbol. While the word 'stress' was first popularized by 'New-Age' thinking, it's now shorthand for all of life's predicaments. It's chic or even *de rigueur* to be stressed. Many individuals seem to want more stress than the next person: 'I can see you are stressed, but if you had my workload and family responsibilities, honestly you would be uber [super] stressed.' The subtext, of course, is that 'I am fundamentally more important than you'. Therefore we are already socially geared towards stress situations within the family.

Stress may also be seen as a male status symbol; as men can no longer deal with the source of stress by killing it or running away from it, they have to perform the alternative – enduring it, for which stamina is needed. Therefore men who have the ability to bear a great deal of chronic stress may be perceived as the most successful, according to

Professor Strepp Porta, professor of endocrinology at the University of Graz.

So, is it everything that is stressful or just some things? Let us take a look.

Which of these is stress?

- You have bought some flatpack furniture for the family home and now have to assemble it.
- A member of the family is getting married and you have been asked to make a speech at the reception.
- You look at the family dog; it is very old, and can hardly walk because of arthritis. Something will have to be done.
- You are responsible for the family accounts and you get a reminder from the Inland Revenue that your tax returns for the past financial year are overdue.
- There are a host of family duties this weekend that require the car, but you feel environmentally guilty for driving these days, and also too weary from the week to really get interested.
- You have started to sneeze and your nose is running.
- Your brother is expecting you for lunch to discuss a problematic business situation in which you're both involved.

The answer: *all* of these are stress.

Yet stress itself is not inherently bad, however; it's how we *interpret* it. Once we have interpreted certain external factors as stressful, they become 'real' – that is, they affect our bodies. And it is our bodies' alarmed reaction to stress that is potentially damaging for us. Our body/mind (I use the term interdependently) is designed to withstand threat of any kind and is on guard against anything hostile to its well-being. However, this does not make us passive in this interplay between external stress and our selves. We can intervene. It is the ability to manage our reactions to the 'external insult' that is key. I will cover this perception skill in some detail in Chapter 4.

Primed for stress

Physiologically, we are primed for stress by a pattern of 'stone-age' reactions that prepare the human organism for physical activity. If you are a cave woman on the savannah, you are better off presuming that the motion you detect out of the corner of your eye is a threat and something to run from, so you get safely back to the family. A rustling in the grass, and a surge of adrenaline prepares you for action.

ᴧ if you are wrong and it turns out to have been just the rustling ves, you are still alive if you acted on your fear. Countless millenniums later, we still presume that, if there is motion just out of our line of sight, it is caused by something – an animal or person (a threat) with the ability to move independently.

A classic experiment by the psychologists Fritz Heider and Marianne Simmel suggested that imputing agency ('I know there is something there'), or attributing meaning to events, is so automatic that people may do it even for geometric shapes. Subjects watched a film of triangles and circles moving around. When asked what they had been watching, the subjects used words like 'chase' and 'capture'. They did not just see the random movement of shapes on a screen; they saw pursuit, planning and escape.

In relation to family stress, what can we take from such an experiment? We can fairly safely extract that our brains are primed to presume and ready to concoct a story. Over aeons of time the human brain has evolved this capacity to impose a narrative, complete with chronology and cause-and-effect logic, on whatever it encounters, no matter how apparently random. So we automatically, and often unconsciously, look for an explanation of why things happen to us. Some refer to this as the *post hoc* fallacy. With this line of reasoning, we convince ourselves that if something happened after an event, therefore it was caused by it: 'I inherited my shyness from my father, therefore I didn't get that job', 'Our family was born unlucky, no wonder I got robbed'. Many superstitions arise from this line of thinking. And superstitions can play their part in family lore, as we explore when looking at family myth in Chapter 3.

In days of yore, stress may have been an adequate reminder that we are alive and wish to remain so (Stone Age woman hotfooting it back to the cave when she heard the leaves rustling), but not so today when you are stuck in the office with charts to read and meetings to rearrange.

Family and forgetfulness

Research suggests that the family is the biggest cause of stress to slightly older women (aged 30–50), whereas study or work is more likely to affect the younger 20–30 age bracket. At 30–50, women are more likely to be coping with a growing range of family responsibilities including young children, older children or teenagers and ageing parents, as well as work. One classic symptom of stress is forgetfulness. Many women with heavy family responsibilities worry that they are losing their minds, or developing Alzheimer's disease, but the truth is probably that they simply have too much to do. In a small but suggestive study, a team of neurologists from the University of Rochester (New York) found that the problem is not really one of impaired memory, but to do with the way that stressed, middle-aged women take in new facts – or rather, don't *learn* new facts. The team found that, instead of forgetting, the women never actually take in the information in the first place – they already have too much on their minds. Spreading your attention too thinly makes it difficult or impossible to encode or take in new information, according to Dr Mark Mapstone and Dr Miriam Weber, memory experts at the University of Rochester's Memory Disorders Clinic. 'And perhaps knowing that their perceived problems with memory do not suggest early dementia might alleviate their concerns and actually improve their functioning – it's one less thing to worry about,' commented Dr Weber.

The researchers concluded, however, that women who feel anxious or depressed shouldn't just put up with this memory problem as something to be expected, but should seek treatment.

Stress and ill health

The medical figures for stress are certainly daunting; in the UK, more than 40 per cent experience adverse health effects from stress, while 75–90 per cent of visits to GPs are for stress-related conditions and complaints. Stress has been linked to the leading causes of death: heart disease, lung ailments, accidents, cirrhosis of the liver, and suicide.

Our 'pathogenic' (which means capable of causing disease) mechanisms to stress include:

- Emotional reactions, such as anxiety, depression, hypochondria and alienation.
- Cognitive reactions, including difficulty in concentrating, remembering, learning new things, being creative, making decisions.
- Behavioural reactions – for example, abuse of drugs, alcohol and tobacco; destructive and self-destructive behaviour, and inhibitions about seeking help.
- Physical reactions such as the neuroendocrine one – this describes

certain cells that release hormones into the blood in response to stimulation of our nervous systems.

- Disruption to the body's immune system.

Armed with this information, clearly we should treat stress and what it does to us as individuals and families with the greatest respect.

Martin once more

Increasingly, the motorway sign has been flashing 'Attention High Winds! Drive Slowly'. Martin slows down as he feels his car being buffeted by the winds on the suspension bridge. He thinks there never used to be high winds every day. As his car veers from a gust of wind he knows this persistently odd weather is global warming. Not something that is in the offing, but a reality that is here. He recalls the last family holiday in France, in the 2003 heat-wave. He can't recall if his children have ever seen snow. Drought orders are now a permanent way of life in the UK. It's here! What kind of future will there be for his kids? He feels himself getting more and more stressed about this imagined future. Look at this, he thinks, observing the endless stream of cars. And he is one of them, so he is guilty too. Not only is he thinking about all his family worries, but the fact that the world is becoming a mess. Apart from the family, he must stop taking on the worries of the world, but he can't help himself, he thinks, as he yanks at his tie.

Are you prone to stress?

Our beliefs, attitudes and values influence how we interpret and react to potentially stressful situations, and a negative interpretation of stressors affects our ability to cope with stress. If we tend to see those situations as threats, pressures, demands or catastrophes, we compromise our ability to cope. The resulting feeling of helplessness sets us up for a variety of unpleasant responses to stress.

Stages of stress

Hans Selye identified three stages in stress. Famous as they now are, it's still worth summarizing them as a useful starting point on stress: a brief alarm period, followed by a prolonged period of resistance, and culminating in exhaustion.

Phase 1 – the alarm phase

Events trigger your body's response to stress – the flight or fight response, a surge of adrenaline and excitement, characterized by such physical changes as quickened heartbeat, rapid breathing, slowed digestion, increased sugar circulating in blood serum, and decreased fat absorption.

Phase 2 – resistance

As the stress continues, the body adapts to the perceived threat and remains in a state of arousal, but we may lose our energy and become run down. As the pressure mounts – or so we perceive it – we may increasingly struggle to meet the various demands we feel are expected of us. Irritability, over-reaction to minor events, inability to cope with routine tasks, and changes in sleeping patterns and behaviour may be observed, both by ourselves and by others.

Phase 3 – exhaustion

Under prolonged stress, if no action is taken, then the body's resources are drained. We can no longer maintain a level of high alert, and exhaustion sets in. We might feel too tired to work or to enjoy life. The stage is set for illness.

Stress signs to look out for

Stress can be expressed in varied fears ('I'm going to lose control'), breathing problems (hyperventilation or rapid shallow breathing), aches and pains such as headaches and lower back pain, or escapist behaviour such as drinking or watching television all the time.

Check your stress

How many of the following statements do you agree with?

- I often feel dizzy, lightheaded or faint.
- I feel tired even when I've had enough sleep.
- I wake up early.
- I often suffer a racing heartbeat and/or palpitations.
- I comfort eat or even binge.
- I feel as though I'm detached from what's going on around me.
- I keep feeling tearful for no real reason.
- My memory has deteriorated.
- I don't feel as if my body is 'real'.
- My usual routine is really tiring, and social events very draining.
- I have trouble sleeping.
- I worry that I have a brain tumour or that I'm going to have a heart attack.

- I suffer digestive problems although my doctor has reassured me there's nothing wrong.
- My performance at work is slipping.
- I drink more than I used to.
- It takes me longer to do routine tasks.
- I seem to get far more minor illnesses than I used to.
- I have problems concentrating; I don't enjoy reading as much as I used to.
- I have panic attacks.
- I have neckache from tense shoulder and neck muscles.
- I don't really want to see people – it takes too much effort.
- I seem to spend my life chasing my tail without getting much done.
- My frustration level seems to be much lower.
- Love and physical contact don't interest me at the moment.
- I am continually on edge and irritable even with my nearest and dearest.
- I get episodes where I feel I can't breathe properly.
- I get more headaches than I used to.

This is a suggested rather than an exhaustive list. Stress can take many forms, physical, mental or emotional. Do check out any worrying symptoms with your doctor and don't assume that it's 'all down to stress'.

Although stress is often present, its specific sources can go unnoticed. There are a myriad family stressors and situations, such as being involved in a family business; being the long-term carer of an elderly parent; and family wills. In some of the following chapters I will look at specific circumstances that cause stress in families.

3

How we interrelate in the family

What will the family think of me?

We may spend a lot of time and energy worrying about what other members of the family think of us. No matter how old we are, what family says to us 'bites' – or what we *think* they say to us. As George A. Miller, the acclaimed professor of psychology at Princeton University, puts it, 'Most of our failures in understanding one another have less to do with what is said and what is heard, than with what is intended and what is inferred.'

I'll be looking at this key variable in family stress – perception – in the next chapter. For now, we will explore the ways in which we may relate to other family members, and how such interrelations contribute to our view of ourselves, and our levels of family stress.

Mary

A mature student, Mary was renowned for a formidable intelligence that she had always secretly doubted. She was now, to everyone's surprise, struggling with her master's degree thesis. This only confirmed Mary's worst fears about her intelligence. It was the reaction of her wider family that caused her most stress. 'Oh Mary, she is the clever one of the family. So bright.' Mary was extremely anxious about the possibility of failing with all the family looking on. She started arguing with her tutors and began to feel paranoid that they were against her because she was a mature student. Each new draft of her thesis was met with more criticism. She felt threatened and exposed. She began to drink coffee late at night to try and do another, then another, draft. Now she was having difficulty in sleeping.

At 3 o'clock in the morning she found herself standing in the bathroom. She suddenly felt light-headed then found she was falling. When she came to, her husband stood her in front of the mirror so she could see the bruise to the side of her head, which he now padded with cotton wool.

Talking later that week with her professor and being honest for the first time about it all, she listened as he recounted the amount of students who over the years had become stressed to breaking point because of academic pressure. 'You mustn't get too stressed about it all' was his sage summing-up.

Family myths

The bright one. The black sheep. The practical but intellectually challenged one. The dancer, the singer, the reader, the engineer. The foundations for how we see ourselves – and others – are laid early.

Sometimes, the main unconscious preoccupations of family members can be condensed into family 'myths' that may maintain the family's psychological stability, and determine family roles. Pioneering family therapist John Byng-Hall has suggested that myths can exert a powerful unconscious influence on the 'life-scripts' of family members, and he outlines how access can be gained to myths through the stories or legends still consciously current in the family.

Assigning 'catch-all labels' to other family members can be the cement that hardens into family myths: 'He has always been a loner, just like his grandad.'

Some family stories, such as those that support isolation, can seem fixed, even having the power to dull a person's awareness of his or her personal strengths.

Colin

I always felt I was 'interesting'. That is how I rationalized being alone. I would sit in bars, sipping away, and comfort myself that I was alone because I was interesting. 'Bit of a loner, is our Colin', my family would explain. I got a kind of 'loner' label which I thought it was right to conform to. Then I started reading and realized that there were other ways. The truth was I had never acknowledged that I was desperately lonely and afraid to risk or trust myself with others because I had no concept of my own value or any personal strength I might have.

A family member's deep belief in his uselessness or unlovability or irredeemable guilt may be a prison. It is important to realize that you can create a better 'story' for yourself, and that such tremendous family tales, these 'home truths', are never final, and possibly not even true at all, however strong their grip on our self-perception and imagination. Indeed, to family members, 'veracity is never the main point – what's important is what could be rather than what actually was,' says Elizabeth Stone, professor of English and author of the classic book *Black Sheep and Kissing Cousins*.

Regardless of whether it's true or not, the so-called family 'truth' (myth) has a unique influence on us, says Elizabeth Stone, 'What the family tells us has a force and power that we never quite leave behind. What they tell us is our first syntax, our first grammar, the foundation onto which we later add our own perceptions and modifications. We are not entirely free to challenge the family's beliefs as we might challenge any other system of belief. And even when we do challenge, we half disbelieve ourselves.'

Family myth, then, sends powerful messages about who each person in the family is, what each member is to do, and how. Such stories, often handed down from generation to generation, offer an explanation of what family members do and how they behave; they help the family make sense of itself and its shared experience. Each family creates its own idiosyncratic or unique genre of storytelling. 'Almost any bit of lore about a family member or experience qualifies as a family story – as long as it is significant and has worked its way into the family canon to be told and retold,' comments Stone.

Take Laura's grandfather, George, for example, who had worked his way into family myth as being a 'gambler'. Laura's grandmother would frequently tell the story of how she came home one day to find that George had sold her beloved horse. Her shock in finding the empty stable, and his laconic explanation that it had been sold to pay his gambling debts, made a long and dramatic story that was told and re-told within the family. Behind this tale lay a whole history of an unsatisfying marriage, entered upon too young; years of poverty and unsatisfactory jobs for George, and finally a move from a beloved area so George could find work in London. The whole thing was a cautionary tale with an underlying motif of poverty and frustration.

Sometimes the stories themselves are hidden or partly 'invisible' (like the iceberg model) and only the effects are seen – those who knew Laura, for example, might have seen only that she was extremely careful with money. They would not have understood her background of poverty and insecurity.

Family stories are of course selective and only some incidents are remembered and preserved; they do not merely bluntly re-tell, but present, embellish and omit to fit the family 'truth'. Typically they may feature the black sheep of the family, often a man (though they may equally feature someone who has led a blameless life).

Nathan had always presented his Uncle Julian as a lovable, charismatic rascal. He would recount stories of his daring exploits as a youth, and how he 'always got away with it' – climbing orchard walls to steal apples and skiving off school to sell them, escaping from the police and, later, arranging dazzling business coups. When Uncle Julian died, Nathan was more shocked and grieved than he would have thought possible. He couldn't believe that this time 'the old rogue hadn't got away with it'. And, a totally different story of Julian's life emerged at the funeral, a story of a devout family man who had worked hard all his life to give his best to his wife and sons. His exploits had sunk without trace.

Family folklore experts Steven Zeitlin, Amy Kotkin and Holly Baker note that 'each narrative becomes not a rehash of an event but a distillation of experience' unique to each family. In other words, 'one Julian for Nathan and his family', and quite another 'Julian for Julian's own family'.

Myths and stories have many functions within a family

- They help define the individual or idiosyncratic identity and nature of a family.
- They lay out family values and ideals, the cultural rules and expectations within the family – what Elizabeth Stone calls 'the decorum and protocol of family life'.
- They contribute to a common family memory, so helping family bonding and strengthening identity.
- They contribute to the family's appreciation of other generations within the family and the community.
- They give interpretations, guidance and warnings for survival in the wider world.
- They help to pass on gender identity. Researchers Barbara Fiese and Gemma Skillman found that sons were more likely to hear stories with themes of autonomy than were daughters, especially with more 'traditional' parents.
- They help shape (or even dictate) personality – the so-called character principle of family stories as noted by family folklore experts members, Steven Zeitlin, Amy Kotkin and Holly Baker.

The first thing to do, then, is to accept that we may not be as free as we would like to be with regard to family, and that even rebellion only has meaning in so far as it relates to the family.

So how do we define our roles and self-images with any objectivity? Perhaps the first step is to identify the myths that are prevalent in our own families, defining 'myths' in line with Stone, who holds that family myths and narratives are a mix of fact and fiction that offer possible, if not always plausible, explanations for emotional calamities within the family. Each family has its own key myths that encompass key themes, events and personalities in the history of each family.

Mary again

Mary felt the pressure more acutely as she always felt she was working to compensate for her slightly younger sister, who, though bright, had dropped out of education and was now working at McDonald's. Mary had unconsciously taken on the burden of trying to gain enough academic success for two to try to make up for her parents' disappointment in her sister. The prevailing 'family story' is about academic success – both her parents had wanted to go to university, but had been prevented by lack of funds and the need to earn a living.

Ian

Ian is a 41-year-old salesman on his way to London to see his mother and extended family. He creases his brow anxiously at the prospect. He finds his family so emotionally raw; they push all the wrong buttons. But his mother is poorly and he hasn't seen her for two months. He thinks of his two brothers and sister, hoping they don't 'start'. He's already wound up and resentful that he has to 'go through all this' to see them – a gruelling, even harrowing journey on the London Underground.

Ian's 'story' about his family is one of stick-in-the-muds, people who have failed to move, and therefore people who have failed to move on in life. He desperately doesn't want to 'go back' to revisit them. As Ian bemoans, 'Why do I have to do this for family?' He is not aware of his body tensing along the spine, or his shoulders bunching up, although he is very aware of the fact that he had two days off work because of being so stressed by his last visit to his family in London.

General family myths

Some of the following myths may apply to your family, some may not:

Everyone should be treated fairly in families

In particular, all siblings should be treated with absolute equality. This is a very hard – and unfair – myth. Even if parents bend over backwards to treat children fairly, there may still be perceived unfairness. Mike always got all of Dad's attention. Mum always had a soft spot for Tom. Some of these myths have a grain of truth, but it's always worth checking the facts.

Dermot always felt he was treated as the baby because he was the youngest of the four, all of whom were much more wealthy than he was. One Christmas, after a few drinks, his older brother confessed that in fact the older siblings all tended to view Dermot as a bit of a star – he was the only one who got to university and was, to coin another myth, 'the brain of the family'. Dermot's brother felt they 'tended to be a bit hard on Dermot' and to take him down a peg or two to keep him in order.

Of course, things may be unfair; you may get the smallest share of money or attention in the family. If talking about it to other family members doesn't help, it might be best to work on expanding your social circle and creating an 'alternative family' (see Chapter 11) of people with whom mutual love and respect is possible, such as friends, partners and in-laws.

You don't have to be on your best behaviour with the family

Well, maybe you don't have to don a suit and tie every time you want to address family members (or maybe you do). However, it is possible to err on the wrong side of sloppy – meaning emotionally rather than sartorially.

Susie was the life and soul of any party and a live wire in the office. Once home, though, she kicked off her shoes, sunk into an armchair, and complained about her day and her lot in general. She seemed to leave her sense of fun at the front door when she came in. Her partner and children became fed up with picking up what was left over from the day.

Important events should be 'perfect'

This includes Christmas, a real emotional minefield for many people (see Chapter 8). Remember, perfection only exists in the advertising world. In real life, the perfect picnic transmutes to a day where you get stuck in traffic, the drinking water has been forgotten, and it buckets down the moment you finally get to your destination. The only real piece of equipment you need to bring on a family outing is a sense of humour.

People in our families should know how we feel and what we need

Well, it would be nice. However, relatives are not clairvoyant by virtue of their family standing. Good communication is at the root of understanding.

No matter how badly family behave, we have to put up with each other

No, actually, we don't. A key way to puncture this myth is to ask yourself if you would put up with bad behaviour if it came from someone who was not a family member, or who was a stranger to you.

Tom's brother, Nigel, always seemed to have something better to do than spend time with Tom and his family. Nigel would make arrangements to play tennis with Tom, or spend Sunday with them and bring the children over, then at the last moment he would cancel. Or Nigel would make promises to Tom's children (to take them out or have them to stay) that he never kept. He was also openly critical of the way Tom was bringing up his children and sometimes quite rude and disdainful about his choices of schools, hobbies and activities for his children. Tom's whole family found this hurtful, and also inexplicable how Tom put up with Nigel's behaviour. 'But he's my brother,' said Tom – until his wife made it quite plain that she was not interested in pursuing this fruitless relationship any longer.

Putting up with someone's selfish or dysfunctional behaviour can actually make things worse. The sad truth is that some people require standing up to, if the other person isn't to allow himself or herself to be emotionally abused. The sharp-tongued mother-in-law, the manipulative and selfish sister, the boorish uncle who insists on telling malicious stories in front of one and all that reflect badly on the family, such relatives do not necessarily have to be endured. It's also important, as with Tom's brother Nigel, to protect any children from negative or unpredictable people. If such people are really unacceptable, look at the advice on dealing with difficult relatives in Chapter 9.

4

How we see family
stress – perception

Pauline Boss, family stress expert, says, 'The family's perception of an event is a powerful, if not the most powerful, variable in explaining family stress.'

What if? What if it weren't really all so stressful after all? What if, instead of walking back into a house full of tension every evening, the breadwinner of the family just came home, put the key in the door, and went and lounged in a favourite armchair with a cup of tea? What if, every time the phone rang, the mother/main carer didn't assume, with a thumping heart, that it was a worried call from the school about some dreadful act by her teenage son? What if every remark from the grandparents wasn't interpreted as a ferocious demand, laden with the subtexts of a lifetime? What if we could escape the 'You always ... you never ... I knew it would be this way with you ... stop being so ...'?

What if, in fact, it weren't really all so stressful – and that we just *think* it is? As stress expert Judith Sedgeman, a professor at West Virginia University, puts it, 'What if there really is no battle to fight, the war is fictional, and we're all scaring ourselves to death over an imaginary enemy?'

This may be something of an over-simplification. However, as the above quotes from family stress experts show, it is how families *interpret* events that is key: not what happens to them, but what they *think* happens to them, and how they incorporate it into their family mythology. As families, and as individuals, as we try to make sense of the world, we don't simply function as isolated entities, but bring to bear a whole host of associations and assumptions for every situation we face. We find our own voices amid a chatter of others. In family life, this chatter is very immediate. Sorting out what we think, from what *they* think, and from what we want them to think, and what they want us to think, is an ongoing and complex process.

Does this mean that each family creates its own world-view? And, perhaps more importantly, is it possible to change it? Yes, and yes, I would say. To put it at its most optimistic and elegant, 'Stress might be regarded as a kind of transaction, or exchange, between families and their external environment. This exchange potentially empowers the individual for it is ultimately his/her thinking that will determine how they respond to potentially stressful external circumstance' (Judith Sedgeman).

From this viewpoint, our knowledge of the world is made up purely through social communication, and reality is made up through consensus (whatever we agree with other people). Meaning, then, is created – agreed, if you like – only in a context of language, and signs flagged up by body language.

Georg Simmel, father of modern sociology, was especially concerned with the wider social construction of attitudes and attributes, linking the individual not just to the family but to powerful cultural discourses that constantly define people's lives.

Simmel saw the family as having a dual role:

1 It offers a training ground where members can, in day-to-day inter-actions and differences with other family members, start defining themselves as individuals and establishing their own personalities.
2 It offers members shelter against the wider outside world until they have developed strength and autonomy enough to cope with it.

So, day-to-day stress needs to be looked at in a wider cultural context than simply what goes on between the walls of 33 Acacia Avenue. Family stress, up to a point, can also be seen as having a useful role in a family context in that it forces individuals to define what they really want and are; the family is a kind of mini-battleground preparing us for the challenges of the wider world. Only up to a point, though!

Family stress and the Great Depression

The idea that perception is key in handling family stress comes from Professor Reuben Hill of the University of Minnesota, whose classic study of families in the Great Depression (1929–38) looked at the ulti-mate stressor, how families coped when they lost their livelihood. In this time of economic blight, cities all around the world were hit hard. Unemployment and homelessness soared. Construction was virtually halted in many countries. Farming and rural areas suffered as prices for crops fell by 40–60 per cent. Yet through this, some families survived intact.

Hill interviewed families living in dire poverty after jobs were lost, and suggested that there are two variables that may buffer the family against family stress:

- Inside the family, in terms of the family's outlook and attitude.
- Outside the family, in terms of the amount of social support available to the family.

Hill suggested that some families had a positive outlook, which increased their ability to accept their circumstances.

The family that sees stress as a challenge, feels confident in its ability to handle stress, has had success in handling previous stressful situations, and has prepared for potential problems, will manage stress more effectively.

Identifying stressors and resources

Stephen F. Duncan, a professor at Brigham Young University, suggests that asking the appropriate questions helps to define and identify both sources of stressing and ways in which you might deal with them, using:

- your resources (such as income, education, determination);
- your coping strategies (how you use your resources);
- your point of view (how you perceive the external stressor event).

Professor Duncan asks us to consider three major issues:

1 What are the major family stressors you are experiencing now?
Marriage
Children
Household management

2 What resources and strategies do you think might help?
Personal
Family
Community

3 What is your specific balancing plan?
What will you do?
When will you do it?
Who will be involved?

The power of perception

Perception is the foundation stone for a host of our reactions. Communication, problem-solving, decision-making and stress management all hang on what individuals and families see and perceive. As well as sensing the world – through sight, sound, touch, taste or smell – we perceive it in that we make some sense or meaning of it. We interpret, make inferences and – most dangerously in relation to stress – draw conclusions.

Whenever we observe another's behaviour, whenever we listen, we always draw some conclusion about what was meant or intended, so we are living our lives with little regard for the subjectiveness with which we view external reality. Yet reality, or at least our individual experience of it, is directly related to our perceptions.

Problems with perception

Obviously, accuracy is of key importance when it comes to perception. But this simple statement is fraught with difficulties. Whose accuracy? Must we agree on a family definition of accuracy too before we can proceed? How do we deal with the unrecognized family myths, the flawed assumptions, the taken-for-granteds?

The idea that reality is largely no more than our perception should make us pause before we make any claims to 'objective truth'. Nevertheless, it behoves us to try and challenge our fixed ideas and conceptual boundaries.

But what might these boundaries be? According to Pauline Boss, there are two key problems with perception which may prevent families resolving stress:

Ambiguity

Ambiguity is when people are prevented from getting accurate facts about a situation affecting them, or when they are confused about the family's membership, roles and rules, and so cannot effectively carry out their daily functions.

Denial

A classic way of dealing with change is a refusal to acknowledge a loss, be it of a loved one, a home or health. Denial is typically the first step in grieving a loss, and can be a way of protecting ourselves while we come to terms with what has happened.

However, denial can be an ongoing protection mechanism that turns into an inability to perceive realistically what is going on.

What influences our interpretations?

How much the event is expected

Stress is often a reaction to the ending of predictability, or when routine is disrupted. Someone living in tune with his or her expectations might have no stress even if the conditions might be interpreted as adverse by someone else. A family may live in comparative poverty, but not be bothered so long as there is enough according to their expectations.

Cultural influences

Culture is well documented as an influence on our perception of our world. A classic example is quoted by Marshall McLuhan in an essay which refers to an educational film on water sanitation in an African village, covering activities such as draining pools, putting away empty tins and so on. When the villagers were asked what they had seen, they replied that they had seen a chicken. The film makers had not even realized that there was a chicken in the film, but, on reviewing it, they found that indeed a chicken passed over one corner of the frame for about a second in a film that lasted around five minutes. Other research suggests that people brought up in the country see a wider and brighter range of colours than do those brought up in town, who perceive grey, browns and neutrals more readily. Again, psychologist Jerome Bruner found that the Chukchee of Siberia had very few words for colours, and were very poor at sorting coloured wools. But they had over twenty-four terms for patterns of reindeer hide, and could classify reindeer far better than the average European scientist, who did not have the same precision in vocabulary in this subject.

Family myth

This has a major effect on how we interpret events (see Chapter 3). Family narratives allow us to make sense of our lives, but can also limit them.

Family practice and learned behaviour

Families practise emotions such as anxiety on a daily basis, and the family emotional dynamic may become set in over-reaction. For example: 'It's happened again! Will this family never learn? I've had enough. I'm off.' Emotional habits are learned and can die hard, as suggested by the work of psychologists Douglas Ellson and Robert Leeper, on the fixation of 'sensory conditioning'.

Past family events and beliefs

Over the years, Patrick has acquired certain assumptions and beliefs about his brother, Alex. Quite genuinely, Alex has decided to turn over a new leaf. However, Patrick now assumes that his new 'considerate behaviour' is just a continuation of conduct that is calculated, as usual, to get a return dividend. 'I know him from old; he is devious, mean and calculating,' says Patrick. What Patrick takes to be true about his brother is not easily shaken. 'Leopards don't change their spots,' is Patrick's final cliché.

Therefore our beliefs reinforce our perceptions and our perceptions reinforce our beliefs. Consequently, we may stay stuck in a cycle of repetitiveness, seeing the world as we have always seen it and living our lives within a very narrow band of possibility. Perhaps Patrick's life would be enriched if he accepted his brother's new behaviour.

If people define situations as real

If people define situations as real, they are real. That is, we agree to define our reality, and take the consequences, both mentally and physically. According to sociologist W. I. Thomas, 'If people define situations as real, they are real in their consequences.' This applies physically. Our mind/body does not differentiate between real and imagined stress. We primates have it tough, more so than in other species. The primitive primate stress response can be set in motion not only by a concrete event, but by mere anticipation (the rustling of the leaves which might signal a predator).

'My family would make anybody stressed'

Stress, then, is only stress if we react to it as such. You might think that this is true up to a point. When we're stressed, it's easy to over-react to little things – such as the annoying letter from an aunt accusing you of not visiting your ageing mother often enough when you've just come back from your third visit that week, or your sister cancelling Sunday lunch yet again, and so on – but to be able to laugh at it ourselves later, when we're calmer. But does this work with the big stressors? A dying parent, a family member who isn't pulling her weight in the family business, an ongoing situation with a mentally ill teenager?

Dermot

I have three siblings all old enough to know better, squabbling like mad over a very insignificant inheritance from our mother. At the same time, they are trying to sell the family business, in which I have an interest, but keep sabotaging the sale at the last minute, usually by inordinate delays or a series of minor niggling demands. My family needs the money from the sale of the business – my two teenagers are about to go to university – and the rest of the family just don't listen whenever I make any suggestions – I might just as well not exist.

Dermot, like many others, sees stress as the result of external insults beyond his control. But it helps to challenge our perceptions – Dermot later realized that petty niggling took place on *both* sides, not just the seller's. However, if it is true that external circumstances do not have any intrinsic capacity to produce stress, and that we don't have to be passive with regard to them, then how do we manage this sort of stress?

Without minimizing Dermot's situation, the effect of stressful situations such as his is influenced, as we have seen, by the person's perception and understanding. This isn't to deny what is going on. The harrowing reality of a dying parent, the deep distress caused by an adolescent 'misbehaving', the blow of redundancy – such life events cannot be 'thought away'.

However, as Hill's study shows (pages 33–4), it remains true that, under staggering blows, some families cope better than others. A family's outlook can vary from seeing life changes as uncontrollable events that spell the beginning of ruin for the family, to seeing them as challenges to be met:

- 'This is a disaster. We will never get over it.'
- 'This has happened to us. We will do what we can. Give it time.'

Families who cope

What are the factors that protect the family unit from having a family crisis?

Hill's theories have since been expanded by Hamilton McCubbin, family stress researcher at the University of Wisconsin, who states that families who do a good job of managing stress have the following characteristics:

They do things as a family

This may take work and organization. When under stress, it is surprisingly easy even for people living under one roof to withdraw from one another, to 'isolate'. It can take planning and effort to ensure families undertake activities together.

They build esteem in one another

Again, it can be easy just to keep silent, or shut off from one another, in a stressful family situation. Making time and space to voice appreciation for one another is important. It is very common for a family member's self-esteem to be affected under stress, and people may need more reassurance and support than usual. Families who do a good job of managing stress take care of themselves physically and mentally.

They reach out to their communities

Families are better able to cope with hard times if they develop social support rather than becoming isolated – meeting new friends, joining clubs, getting involved in community projects, and so on.

They enjoy their chosen lifestyle

A feeling of being in control is important when managing stress. If people feel they have chosen their lifestyle, rather than having it imposed on them, they are more likely to cope with the ups and downs of that lifestyle. For example, someone who has moved to a town she dislikes because of her husband's job may not be as resilient under stress as someone who is living where she would like to live.

They actively reduce tension and conflict

They employ a range of tension-reducing devices to ward stress off, such as exercise, relaxation, a positive outlook, and keeping involved in activities.

To these factors, we could add these:

They practise pragmatic truth

By that, I mean using truth for its perceived usefulness in dealing with experience. 'The family are doing their usual dance over the sale of the business and I suspect that they have scared off many genuine purchasers. As I'm not involved in the day-to-day running of it, I don't know the truth and may never know it, but I will be pragmatic about it so that I can move on.' Newtonian science may be a flawed theory, but it got us to the moon!

They agree to differ

The Smiths couldn't agree on a place to move to: town, country, seaside, abroad? They agreed to differ on the area, and instead focused on what they wanted from a move – a better environment, larger garden, and closer access to Mr Smith's work. The area then sorted itself out naturally. In a stress-inducing family disagreement, fortunately we are not in a court of criminal law.

They control their moods

We are all affected by the moods of others, and they in turn are affected by ours. Homeostasis is the word we use for a living being's self-regulation of its internal environment. It also adjusts to the external environment. As we spend a great deal of time with our families, our homeostasis, our emotional temperature, is affected by them. This is neatly displayed by the following example.

While working on the design of the pendulum clock in 1656, Dutch scientist Christian Huygens found that if he placed two unsynchronized clocks side by side on a wall, they would slowly synchronize to each other. In fact, the synchronization was so precise that not even mechanical intervention could calibrate them more accurately. Equally, when the brain is presented with a rhythmic stimulus, such as a drum beat for example, it responds by synchronizing its own electric cycles to the same rhythm. This is commonly called the Frequency Following Response (or FFR). The same concept can be applied to nearly all mental states, including concentration, creativity – and moods. This may explain why, when Dad or big sister is in a mood, everyone else feels on edge. Family members' moods may emanate to us; and ours to them. This doesn't mean we should necessarily put up with someone else's continued bad temper, but it may be worth biting our tongues sometimes over more trivial matters.

Changing your perception

This takes practice, but is much easier if you make a decision to put yourself and your health first, and to stop trying to change other family members, or indeed to expect more of them than your experience would suggest. There are some practical suggestions for changing the way you interact with family members in Chapter 9. People often find that it is when they start acting differently that their perception changes. Take the bull (alias nasty Uncle Phillip) by the horns and he may well dwindle into a harmless sheep.

How we see things

'Funny you should say that, because I didn't see it like that at all.'
    'But it's plain as the nose on your face.'
    'It might be to you, but not to me.'
    'Oh I give up, you're blind.'

How is it that others just don't see our point of view? How can they be so blind? What is the physiology of how we see things? But how do we or any other living creatures see, for example, the phenomena of colour? A bee sees a 'yellow flower' in ultraviolet wavelengths. A bat will experience the flower as the echo of ultrasound. If I were able to look at the brain of any reader, I would not find any image of a yellow flower. So how do we tell it is a 'yellow flower'?

We do so by consensus. If we care to delve into contemporary research in human perception, we find the suggestion that 80 per cent of what we see in the external world is the result of internal assumptions and beliefs.

What if we could realign our intentions, reframe our analysis, and re-define our perceptions? Could we do this and, if so, how? To answer that question it is worth looking at how our brains have developed and are developing.

The reptilian, limbic and neocortex parts of the brain

Many of us live our lives shuttling back and forth between two apparently different identities that often conflict with each other. Our rational self tells us we need to establish a mature relationship with our parents or siblings, while our emotional self has us indulging in the same old rows and the same negative thinking.

We can understand more about why people struggle with integrating their emotions and intellect by looking at the structure of our total human intelligence. Science currently tells us that as a result of millions of years of evolution, each human being is now the owner of an intelligence made up of three different brains, each performing different functions.

Just as when we install updates to our computer, and maybe end up with a discrepancy between old and new systems, we sometimes seem to have a mismatch between the older parts of the brain that govern emotion, and the newer intellectual responses.

The reptilian brain

This brain controls core life functions such as heartbeat and breathing.

The limbic (mammalian) brain

This brain appeared after millions of years of evolution, and controls our emotions. One of its purposes is to keep us close to those who are essential to our survival. It could be called our 'relationship' brain.

The neocortex (rational) brain

This brain deals with reason and speech – our 'reasonable' brain.

'Relationship brain' versus 'reasonable brain'

The problem is that the neocortex has little if any true understanding of emotions; an intellectual understanding of our behaviour patterns will not necessarily help us change them. We live as mammals, in terms of how well we relate to others; our mammalian 'relationship' brain, which we tend to ignore in favour of the more 'reasonable' neocortex, is always popping up.

When considering family, where primitive emotions tend to be dominant, it's important to be aware of how these different brains function, and to realize that we have other options than simply reacting 'from the gut' or, if you like, the mammalian or limbic brain. Next time you want to blow your top with those difficult family members, count to ten and give your neocortex a chance to kick in!

5

Family businesses

The American Beat poet Allen Ginsberg used to joke that poetry was 'the family business'. A look at this statement in *Family Business: Two Lives in Letters and Poetry*, edited by Michael Schumacher, demonstrates an enviable working relationship between Allen Ginsberg and his father Louis, also a poet. As well as spirited arguments, the correspondence also demonstrates mutual respect and affection, honesty and pride in each other's poetic achievements – a winning recipe for any family business.

It would seem, however, that this mix is rare. Businesses that are family owned or controlled account for three-quarters of companies in the UK, and employ more than half the workforce in the private sector. In the USA, there are more than 200,000 private companies with revenues over $5,000,000, the vast majority of which are family owned or controlled. Yet it is estimated that a great proportion of family firms do not succeed into the second generation, and 90 per cent do not continue into a third generation of family ownership or management. So why do so many family businesses fail?

Surveys have shown that business consultants present good business plans to family-run businesses, but fail to take into account individual family dynamics.

The generation gap

Jack

'The problem is my son never grew up understanding the advantage of disadvantage,' says Jack, founder of a chain of boutiques now co-owned and managed by his family. Jack is of the generation who counts the paperclips, and hopes to pass this on to Neal, his eldest son. 'At least when I'm gone there will be someone taking care of the family shop.' But Jack is still around and Neal, his favourite – much to the resentment of the other family members – runs the family business as if it were his own fiefdom.

Jack kept count of the paperclips in the early years because he had to be very cost conscious. He cares deeply about his adult children, but they're tough to deal with. Come to that, so is Jack. He never listens to others because he assumes he already has the right answer, '... after all, it worked for me. That's how I built up this business.'

Jack adds, 'My children have had it so easy. Sometimes I wonder just what kind of world they are living in.'

One business, two generations

Well, they probably *are* living in a different world. When two family generations talk to each other, they are speaking from different frames of reference. In a family-controlled enterprise, the senior generation has usually experienced far more, simply by virtue of age. However, this is less important than the intergenerational difference. The son, for example, thinks differently, not just because he is less experienced with business or life than his father or mother, but because his generation looks at the world through a different prism. It's a common problem that might be summed up thus:

- Typical parent profile might be: cautious, mean/stingy, conservative, traditional, secretive.
- Typical child profile might be: risk-oriented, keen on capital outlay – especially new technology.

Family style

Businesses bring out the essence of a family. 'Successful family businesses come from well families,' as one family business expert said. Some family businesses also show up dysfunction, greed and lack of generosity or vision. Other specific problems may include:

- Rivalry between siblings – for example, one may feel he is working harder than the other.
- Different approaches by siblings, as well as between generations.
- Children who don't want to join the family business.
- Children who may want to join the family business but are unsuitable, or unwilling to pull their weight.
- Squabbles about shares between siblings, especially if some are more active in the business than others.

'Position nepotism'

Birth order, or 'position nepotism', is one possible problem: the 'older brother' or 'older sister' syndrome in which the eldest child may be viewed as more powerful, more special or more entitled, due to their birth order, to be at the head of the pack.

Paul

Paul is Jack's youngest son, and gets special treatment because his mother dotes on him. So a family blind eye is turned when he jets off to Paris, to do some 'research' on other boutiques – that is, taking French models out to dine in fancy Parisian restaurants. Although he does take in the odd exhibition too, seeing himself as a bit of an 'arty writer', Paul makes no real contribution to the growth of the business. His mother's affection enables this kind of behaviour. So while Father dotes on the eldest, Neal, the mother indulges the youngest, Paul. How does Franky, the middle son, feel? He feels left out, resulting in him being livid with rage most of the time. Because of Franky's resentment of the preferential treatment his two brothers receive, he has gathered the family nickname of 'Furious Franky'.

Now Paul is getting married. Family alarm bells ring. Is she the right choice, will she pose a risk to the business?

A marriage can be a key event in a family business, sometimes posing a threat to existing loyalties. Other dynamics can cause stress too, such as inter-family fraternizing. Some people prefer to socialize with certain family members, but not others. Or the opposite – some people never get along well with other members of the family. These feelings, both positive and negative, invariably spill over into the work setting. Such wider family behaviour can be intense, non-collaborative and, at times, destructively competitive.

Minimizing family stress

Fortunately you can minimize the stress of working with your relatives by following universal business rules:

- Treat family fairly. Family members who work in the business should be as competent and experienced as non-family staff, and promotions and salary increases should be based on concrete and clearly seen skills and abilities, not favouritism. Don't let the business be a refuge for family lame ducks; do make use of any special skills family members may have.
- Following on from this, family members should have learned the job thoroughly, perhaps by spending time in each department, or creating a new and separate line of business. Many business experts recommend a period spent working away from

the family firm to build up self-confidence and a wider range of experience.

- Put business roles and relationships in writing, with outside professional advice.
- Communicate, communicate, communicate. Secrecy can ruin a business, as can squabbles. Some differences of opinion and problems are inevitable. Have a formal weekly meeting as the forum to discuss difficult issues.
- Some families feel it is breaking a family rule to ask for outside help or advice, but there may be times when it pays dividends – that is, getting expert tax advice, outside arbitration to resolve disputes, or just fresh ideas. Families can sometimes become too insular. Success can also isolate a family, and outside help may be valuable in helping resolve entrenched family disputes that may have grown with the business.
- Be proactive – don't wait until there is a crisis because family issues are affecting the overall productivity and profitability of the businesses. Tackle problems early, with outside help if necessary.
- Stay neutral. A common trap is placing too much emphasis on family and not enough on business. Relatives may have grown up together, played together, loved and hated one another, but the workplace is not an environment in which to play out or resolve childhood or adult dramas. The ideal is to interact with other relatives in the same neutral manner you'd use with any colleague. Neutrality is a good basis for a family business plan.
- Set boundaries. Try not to talk shop outside business hours or at family gatherings.

Succession plans: monarchs, generals, governors and ambassadors

The above phrase was coined by Professor Jeffrey A. Sonnenfeld, at the Yale School of Management, and his colleague P. L. Spence to describe different styles of leadership in family businesses. When the 'king' has to step down is a crucial and often difficult time for most family businesses, and preparing younger family members for leadership is one of the most challenging tasks faced by chief executives.

It is essential to have a proper succession plan. The Department of Trade and Industry estimates that about 100,000 businesses collapse each year when their owners retire or move on without an effective succession plan in place. Planning ahead should be done several years in advance, but in real life it is often left to a few months. This means that owners are effectively throwing away the achievements of a lifetime, according to the accountancy network Stoy Hayward's BDO Centre for Family Business (<www.bdo.co.uk/cf>). Stoy Hayward identifies the following barriers to planned succession by business founders:

- The fear of death
- Reluctance to release control and power
- Threat to personal identity
- Bias against planning
- Inability to choose among children
- Fear of retirement
- Jealousy and rivalry.

One of the tools employed by Stoy Hayward, for example, is an ethical will, a document allowing the older generation to pass on advice and experience. (An ethical will is also increasingly being used by family members as a way to share values and experience with family members – see Chapter 11.)

Optimizing the chances of a smooth succession

- Create a succession plan well in advance – don't wait until there is an emergency or illness strikes.
- Be realistic when appointing a successor, taking the younger generation's real capabilities (and wishes) into account. The one who inherits the business should be doing so because of experience and ability, not because of who they are.
- Hand over power gradually as the younger generation learns the ropes, ensuring the successor has the right experience, including, if relevant, time spent elsewhere.
- Give scope for the entrepreneurial spirit and allow autonomy in terms of a separate project or a new line of business – for example, offering meals in the family-run hotel.
- Be willing to be educated about new technology.
- Think about the future ownership of the business, particularly if shares will be spread around the family.
- Keep things professional and try not to get into emotional family disputes.
- Get proper legal and financial advice throughout.
- Ensure the handover is clear-cut – the retiring 'king' should try not to offer help afterwards unless asked.

6

Carers

Many people are frightened of the responsibility of caring for a loved one, and rightly so. The informality of the role, the lack of training available for carers, not knowing what services are available, not even knowing what kinds of questions to ask of potential service providers – all these things generate stress. Couple this with the guilt that often arises when the dutiful carer, realizing that the task is too overwhelming, must bring 'strangers' into the care plan, and the stress is compounded.

Who does the caring?

Nearly six million people in the UK are carers, most of them women, but the figure also includes men and young carers (that is, carers under 18, of whom there are estimated to be up to 50,000). Whether you are looking after someone with a disability or illness, or someone who is becoming old and frail, caring can be extremely stressful, not just for the carer but for the whole family.

Nearly half of all carers juggle their role with paid work, while some have to balance the demands of 'caring' with bringing up their own young family. Caring may involve long hours – a survey carried out for the Princess Royal Trust for Carers showed that nearly a quarter of carers work 50 hours a week. It may also involve getting up in the night, not just once, but several times; gruelling physical work such as lifting, bathing and dealing with incontinence; tussling with authorities to try and obtain support and services; and limited opportunities for time off or holidays. There may also be significant financial problems if you have had to give up work to cope with caring.

Caring may put an enormous strain on a marriage or partnership, and also on relationships with other members of the family, including any young children. Being part of the 'sandwich generation' – that is, chronologically sandwiched between generations – can involve a stressful tug of loyalties.

Disagreements among family about who should do the caring, or for how much of the time, may be another source of stress. A classic case is when someone gets landed with the caring just because she or he is geographically nearest to the person who needs care; or, in some cases, 'has always got on best' with Mum, Dad, or whoever it is who needs the care. Conversely, of course, there may be the situation where siblings are 'shut out' from caring, however unconsciously, by the person who has assumed the competent carer's role. As ever, previous and existing family dynamics continue to dominate the scene.

Just over half of carers – 52 per cent – have been treated for stress because of their caring role, according to a study called 'Ignored and Invisible?', carried out by Carers UK. Many more carers suffer stress but never get as far as telling their doctor – if only because they feel there just isn't time to go. Another study, 'In Poor Health: The Impact of Caring On Health', also from Carers UK, found that carers providing high levels of care were twice as likely to suffer ill health as non-carers; and, if they didn't get a break, twice as likely to suffer from mental health problems.

Other research backs up these findings. The stress of caring for a person with dementia has been shown to affect the carer's immune system for up to three years after their caring ends. Family carers who provide care for 36 or more hours a week are far more likely than non-carers to ex-perience depression or anxiety – if you are caring for a partner, the rate is six times higher; if it's for a parent, the rate is twice as high. Intensive family caring may also result in insomnia, hypertension, frequent colds and flu, back injuries, body pain, headaches, recent weight loss or gain, and chronic fatigue. If too many demands are placed on the care-giver, feelings of guilt, resentment and exhaustion can be the result.

A key point is that many carers are unaware of just how much help is available, or don't know how to access it. Carers in the UK are esti-mated to save the UK economy an incredible £57 billion a year – the equivalent of a second National Health Service. However, there is a great deal of financial and practical support around; for more advice, see *The Complete Carer's Guide*, by Bridget McCall (Sheldon Press 2007).

Sarah

However, it's not all bad news. As with so many other women, the role of carer fell on Sarah simply because she was the only female in the family, but, despite natural negative feelings, she concluded that the experience was a very positive one:

Sarah had been assigned to look after her ageing mother by her siblings almost by default. There was little discussion and no family agreement on this, Sarah was hardly consulted, and it was just assumed that she would do this harrowing job.

Sarah's mother had been a lifelong smoker. She had already had two operations for lung cancer, and a third one was not possible in her current frail state. Now she refused to go into a nursing home, because she knew she would never come out alive. And so it fell on Sarah's shoulders to wash and clean her mother.

Although she loved her mother, Sarah could not help but feel a deep resentment as the days wore on. However, she now feels that was the most rewarding experience of her life – just to be there for her mother up to her death.

Sarah's story highlights some possible benefits of being the family carer:

- Your life can be enriched by helping others.
- You experience a closer relationship with those you care for.
- Your children will learn to deal with care, and caring issues, by example.

Pet dogs reduce the stress of caring

Many studies have shown that pets can help to reduce blood pressure; now research by Dr Karen Allen at the University of Buffalo shows specifically that a pet dog can help reduce hypertension in carers. People caring for a brain-injured partner were shown to have just one-fifth the rise in blood pressure during stressful, caregiving activities compared to those without dogs. And, when people without dogs got one six months into the study, their average blood pressure and heart rate during stressful situations dropped to match that of the initial group.

Life on hold

Most family members readily jump in to help a loved one and put their own lives on hold. Often, though, it's with the expectation that they won't be carers for longer than two years. In fact, the average length of time spent on care-giving is usually much longer, as Liz found.

Liz
When my husband, Rob, asked if his father could stay with us, I was happy to welcome him but assumed it would be temporary. At that time he was frail, but well, and relatively independent – he could get

around and feed himself and was lively company. However, once he was in our house, we never felt that we could ask him to go, or send him to a nursing home, which we couldn't afford anyway. He had been such a fine, proud man in his prime, so at first I didn't mind looking after him. I had a part-time secretarial job at a local architect's office, but as he got weaker I had to give that up.

A year later the situation had changed dramatically. I had to get up during the night to turn him over; and he also needed help with feeding, medications and toileting.

To be honest, after five years, his passing was a relief, but in some ways it was too late. Rob and I drifted apart. I never thought that would happen – we had been married for 31 years. Now I wonder who is going to look after me, when my times comes. My family are scattered over the country.

I also feel that my relationship with my grown-up children suffered in those years, especially the eldest who had two babies in that time. I wasn't as available to support her as I might have been. I think about it a great deal.

Coping with caring

If you are an overwhelmed carer, have a look at the suggestions for coping with stress in the later parts of this book (Chapters 10, 11 and 12). There is plenty you can do to start putting yourself first and giving yourself, as well as others, some care.

In addition:

- Call your social services if you haven't already done so and make an appointment to see what help is available. You can ask for an assessment to be made that takes into account your needs as well as the needs of the person being cared for.
- Don't complicate caring by worried or guilty thoughts. Substitute stress-neutral thoughts. For example, 'worried thought': 'I am abandoning my mother by leaving her in a day centre.' 'Stress-neutral thought': 'It is difficult to leave my mother, but I know that the staff will take care of her needs.'
- Discuss matters with the whole family – don't let the chief responsibility fall on you without it being clear exactly what everyone else is prepared to do. Do all you can to enlist the help and support of family. If necessary, set limits and make it quite clear that you are doing so. A typical scenario is where one sibling doesn't want a parent to go into a home, but is unwilling or unable to provide

the extra care that will help keep him or her at home, and expects another sibling to do it all.

- Talk to other care-givers. Look for local carers' associations or contact a national support group such as Carers UK (CarersLine 0808 808 7777; web address <www.carersuk.org>).
- Make time for yourself a priority. You must get adequate breaks, time away from home, and holidays. Do use outside help to achieve this.

7

Deaths, funerals and wills

The death of a family member affects the entire family structure, the family's identity, and the family's purposes. All facets of the family structure can become imbalanced. Death is what Reuben Hill referred to as a 'crisis of dismemberment', an apt term for the loss of a part of the family body. If an older member dies, the entire generational balance has to be adjusted as people 'move up' a generation and take on new roles; for example, Paul, who spent his life as 'the youngest', found himself among the oldest generation of his family when both his parents died. There was a further readjustment too when his oldest brother Neal also passed away.

Paul
When I last saw Neal I was reminded of something I had read or seen – it was this image of people gathered at the shore before the departure of a ship: you know, people have more than ever to say to one another at this point and there is this need to say something meaningful, but the words don't come, so there are tears. For you know the future presses, so greedy is it, so certain of its prey. So you sob a little and hold him in an awkward embrace. And then he was gone.

The family's ability to adapt to a death is affected by a variety of factors, according to Professor Colleen Murray at the University of Nevada. These include at what point the death occurred in the life-cycle, and the nature of the death itself. Also, if families have other stressors, then if the person was central to the family's operations, or if there was conflict with the person who has died, the family will be more vulnerable.

Professor Froma Walsh, of the University of Chicago, and Professor Monica McGoldrick, of the University of Medicine and Dentistry, New Jersey, have proposed that to adapt to the loss of their family member, the family must:

- Recognize the loss as real. To do this, family members must share emotions and thoughts with one another. Grief is an isolating experience.
- Reorganize the family system. As indicated above, the family system

53

is destabilized by the loss, and a new order needs to be established. This can be a disruptive, even chaotic, process marked by disagreement and outright battles as family members reorganize and absorb the roles and tasks of the person who has died.

- Accept differences of opinion and grieving styles, and be more tolerant of behaviour at this time.
- Re-invest in the family and get back to a new 'normality'. This reclaiming of a normal life can also cause conflict as it can feel like an abandonment of the deceased loved one by some family members. Again, it is important to accept differences in the pace as well as the style of grieving family members.
- Communicate openly, and allow other family members to talk about the deceased.

Walsh and McGoldrick point out that the grief and reorganization process takes time, given the needs and limited resources of family members after a loss. Rituals such as funerals, religious rites, or even family holiday rituals, can help.

Funerals

It is an unfortunate fact that family funerals often bring out the worst in family members. Some of the most long-lasting family arguments have started at a funeral, with anything from squabbles over the hierarchy of seating arrangements, to arguments about expressions of faith, to the venting of long-entrenched differences, and even, childish though it sounds, feuding and rivalry about the sincerity of grief. I have actually seen an e-mail from one sibling to another that accuses him of 'crocodile tears' after the death of a sibling, given the previous family quarrels. Past feuds do not of course get rid of the need for grief; they simply complicate it. In this case, the oldest son was not asked to deliver the address. He was not slow to express his fury at the reception after the service. Another family member came over to stave off the brewing row, and got embroiled. By now, we are not far off a comic scene.

Funerals are occasions when family members have probably not seen one another for some time, and there is naturally going to be tension. But why are funerals so often the occasion for sources of contention? Do the resentments of a lifetime find an outlet at this time of intense emotion? Perhaps it is the invidious positioning of bereaved people. We are placed between the living and the dead in what might be termed a condensed form of ritualized experience. This suspension of our usual roles is stressful. Funerals are rituals and our individual behaviour is regulated by the social context of a family system that is itself embedded in and mutually regulated by wider community and cultural contexts. So we must act our roles of sad or grief-stricken under the frown of these wider cultural contexts.

The funeral process has changed over time; the change of titles from 'undertaker' to 'funeral director' has been perhaps the largest single clue to the functions the industry now sees itself as 'performing'. You could argue that the funeral 'director' is controlling a dramatic production in which we have been assigned roles. The point here is that much of our behaviour is ceremony for we are being asked to publicly 'perform' too. Some of this ceremony that we are required to 'perform' is worth an overview for it is revealing that our funeral customs have their historical basis in pagan ritual. In this sense, we may be partaking of a wider family function than that of the immediate family; we could be said to be taking on tribal roles.

For example, the viewing of the body by friends and relations before the burial, to which some people subscribe, was originally an obligation, in order that those who were present at the death might clear themselves of any suspicion of foul play.

Our modern mourning clothing came from the custom of wearing special dark garb as a disguise to hide identity from returning spirits. Pagans believed that returning spirits would fail to recognize them in their new attire and would be confused and overlook them. Covering the face of the deceased with a sheet stems from pagan tribes who believed that the spirit of the deceased escaped through the mouth. Wakes come from ancient customs of keeping watch over the deceased hoping that life would return. The lighting of candles comes from the use of fire in attempts to protect the living from the spirits.

However, people are increasingly evolving more creative and modern ways of dealing with funerals and the death process. See *How to Approach Death*, by Julia Tugendhat (Sheldon Press 2007).

Delivering the tribute

There are few occasions more emotive than being asked to deliver a tribute at a family funeral. The spectacle of the bereaved one standing before the other mourners, too overcome with grief to speak, is one we have probably all seen – or have even been in the role ourselves. On such occasions, it may help to remember that short and simple is often best, and it is no shame to read from a set of notes.

Tributes come in all shapes and sizes. Some are wildly unlike the deceased, others may be used as a chance to score concerning family issues and rivalries, provoking further family quarrels, or even to make startling revelations about the dearly departed.

More seriously, a funeral is a core event for any family. The ceremony allows people to remember and honour their loved one; it serves as a gathering place for family and friends to give one another emotional support. It encourages mourners to face the reality and pain of their loss and express their thoughts and feelings.

Wills

Monica's grandmother
Monica's Italian grandmother was sitting surrounded by her ten children and countless grandchildren at a family celebration. The local priest, who was visiting, asked her how the family managed to be so happy and contented, all the generations sitting together enjoying themselves, with no quarrels. 'It's easy when you have no money,' replied the matriarch. 'For years I wondered what she meant,' said Monica. 'Surely life was hard enough with no money? Finally I realized she meant that there was nothing to quarrel over.'

Monica's grandmother died in her nineties. The house she rented disappeared with her and she left few material possessions, though typically ensuring that she had saved enough to pay for the funeral costs. And every year the family still celebrate the birthday of this much-loved and still missed family figure.

Family, death and money form a lethal cocktail for some families, and family inheritance disputes are reported to be rising. To some extent, this may be because there is more at stake. Today's 'baby boomers' – those born during the economic prosperity following the Second World War – stand to inherit more, especially as the rise in property values means that estates become more valuable. There are millions of baby boomers – almost one in five people in the UK is aged over 65. UK baby boomers have more investments, disposable income and higher pension wealth in real terms than any other generation has had at retirement age, according to research by Halifax Financial Services. And in the USA, baby boomers are due to inherit some $10.4 trillion, according to a Cornell University report. More than half of all wealth in the USA is held by people over the age of 55 – that is, 37 per cent of the population. Baby boomers may also have more debt and a higher cost of living, especially costs such as university fees and, in the USA, healthcare costs.

In addition, over the last two decades family relationships have become much more complicated as a result of the ever-increasing number of remarriages and 'blended' (stepchildren through second marriages) families.

Small reason, then, that lawyers are reporting more infighting over who gets what – nearly one-third of all baby boomers have already been involved in a dispute over an inheritance. But there is almost always more to such a family war than money, and the size of the estate does not necessarily mirror the size of the dispute. Many quarrels over wills accurately reflect family relationships while all parties were alive, and may have their roots in old jealousies and rivalries, greed and bitterness. When a parent has died, it's easy at such a vulnerable time to feel hurt by the provisions of a will, or to feel that a parent has treated one sibling better than another, or continued an age-old preference: 'She always was the favourite.' Many adult children read a will as a parent's last words, with rewards bestowed upon them as a measure of their love; or as a declaration of their innermost, 'real' feelings towards them, without taking into account that wills do not really tell the whole story. For example, some wills may leave less to one child than another, but omit to explain that this was because the parents paid university fees for this child, or helped that person buy a house. An ethical will (see Chapter 11), or a simple letter, may help to prevent this kind of bitter misunderstanding.

Nick, Anthony and Maria inherited their father's estate, but Nick inherited less. Nick had had a drugs problem in his late teens, and his parents had paid hefty clinic fees to help him recover, whereas the other two had needed no such extra expenditure.

Yet another situation is where a partner will push a spouse into a family feud. Susan had spent most of her adult life in New Zealand and had seen very little of her family. When her parents died within three months of each other, she was content to receive a relatively small inheritance – after all, she had effectively ignored them for nearly twenty years. Her husband, however, felt that Susan had been slighted and ignored in her turn by the family, and generally undeservedly treated as the 'black sheep', and wanted her to have a larger slice 'so that justice could be done'.

As lawyers will tell you, it is easier to avoid a dispute than to resolve one – though because of the factors outlined above, family conflicts over inheritances are sometimes inevitable.

The real problem with such family disputes is that, if bitter, the battle for the money may be won, but part or all of the family lost. In the process, there may be just a few too many harsh words exchanged. It's not unknown for lawyers actually to put people in such disputes in separate rooms while endeavouring to sort them out, for fear of individuals' hurtful comments truncating the day before any progress has been made.

Dying intestate

However hurtful or unfair the provisions of a will may appear to be, an even more common situation is when there is no will at all. Despite a steady stream of advice from the government, lawyers and other bodies, a staggering two out of three people in the UK die intestate (i.e. without having made a will) – the problem often being that someone doesn't want to think about his or her death in advance.

Another problem is a homemade will, which can easily be contested if just one family member becomes difficult.

Moira

Moira, the powerful matriarch of a very successful immigrant Irish family, caused ripples of shock throughout the clan when she died without leaving a will – or so her carer, her daughter Sandy, claimed.

As his mother had mentioned her will to him many times, Hubert, the youngest, remained convinced that there had in fact been a will and that his mother had disposed of it under the 'undue influence' of her carer, his older sister, Sandy.

The dispute over the estate became more embittered, until it was of Greek proportions. Finally the family members would not talk to one another and would only communicate by letter. Hubert fought to become the administrator of the will, and at the time of writing the feud over the will is still in dispute.

As well as money squabbles, though, arguments over so-called trivia often wreak just as much emotional havoc in an inheritance dispute, such as what happens to Mum's collection of antique lace that she inherited from her own mother, Uncle William's vintage toy train collection, or the pile of manuscripts that Dad never managed to get published. Wills are also about recognition. The same applies after a death when the relatives are less close than parents – grandparents, aunts, even siblings. Here there may be little money involved, but a great deal of old affection, which, the survivors may feel, is by no means recognized after a death.

Helen and Rose had always been close to their grandmother, who promised them five or six antique rings when she died. In the event, their aunt, who was their grandmother's main carer, disposed of all her effects without taking any such wishes into account, and reputedly ignoring an informal will or letter stating these.

Mementos of the deceased have far more value than their financial worth, and the tact and sensitivity with which families handle them can be a key part in coming to terms with the loss of a significant family member.

As the above case histories show, the problem for a family of *not* leaving a will can be immense. Fortunately, not everyone is like the family of Helen and Rose.

Gordon had four children, who followed his will amicably and obediently. The youngest, John, who was a Buddhist monk, took only his father's shaving brush to remember him by.

Claudine's dying father, who was French, called his three daughters to his bedside and told them they would find 'it' behind some bricks in the living room, to the left of the chimney breast. 'And enjoy it!' he added. After the funeral, when the bricks were removed, sure enough, there among the dust and mice droppings were the bundles of cash. The money was evenly divided up on the spot and they went off to the pub. Not a harsh word was ever spoken about it.

The executor

If, like Hubert, you find yourself the administrator of a will, be advised that you may face a long period of red tape, battles with family members and even lawsuits. However, in less choppy family waters, the executor's job typically lasts from a few months to two years. If you're asked to be a successor trustee for a living trust, your function will be much like that of an executor. Executors' duties include:

- Locating and valuing the dead person's assets.
- Finding and paying any creditors.
- Filing estate tax returns if the estate is large enough.
- Making sure any remaining property and money are transferred to the person's heirs according to the terms of the will or living trust.

Note: It is important that all inherited money is declared to the Inland Revenue.

8

Christmas, holidays and weekends

Christmas

Figures from the National Association of Travel Agents for 2006 show that around three million UK citizens leave their native shores at Christmas (an increase of one million on the previous year) to spend Christmas abroad. Some go in search of snow; some are looking for sun; and some – though the statistics don't say so outright – are trying to get away from the family stresses and associations that over the years have become just too turgid and depressing to bear any longer.

For many families, Christmas wouldn't be Christmas without the good old traditional family squabble. The stage is set by the run-up to Christmas, two of the most tense weeks in the year, when days are dark and short, and temperatures low. Seasonal affective disorder (SAD) may affect some with depression and lethargy. Crowded shops, commercial pressures, money worries, end of year deadlines, workloads and ill health are among the realities that can contribute to family stress. Against that, we are bombarded with images of happy families: Christmas trees, snow, candles, carols, gifts, seasonal sights and sounds and smells, and a general heightened emotional state of arousal, all guaranteed to arouse a mixture of nostalgia and desolation.

One in five of us becomes stressed during the festive season, according to a survey by the mental health charity Mind, who have found that Christmas is as common as relationship problems and health worries for causing stress. The Samaritans' helpline advisers expect 10 per cent more calls – around 100,000 – during the holiday period, and the suicide rate reaches its peak in January. Yet another survey showed that 41 per cent of us find the Christmas season and family get-togethers to be somewhat or very stressful.

So what happened to the Dickensian Christmas of cheer and goodwill? Apart from the fact that our current view of Christmas was indeed created almost singlehandedly by Dickens, it seems that the Christmas season has an energy of its own that can all too often just sweep families along with it. At Christmas, families are already on edge, and increased demands on time and energy can sap the strength of the most resilient family. Simply by opening your home to your wider family, you're exposing it to all manner of psychodrama, from long-standing sibling rivalries to deep-seated grudges and poor self-esteem. It's a time when you may feel more acutely any losses in the previous year, such as deaths, divorce, broken relationships or lost jobs, not to mention old family hurts.

It's unfortunate, but true, that for many families Christmas evokes memories of that family row as well as that jumper and those socks. At the annual family gathering, you are likely to meet all those family members who make you feel a touch nervy: your sister's husband, who hasn't deigned to talk to you all year; the family members who always remember the hurt of 20 years ago; the family alcoholic; the family bully. All the funny hats at the family reunion can't mask the bitterness. And if we care to peep in, already there is a blazing row going on between Uncle Luke and Uncle Sebastian:

'You are left of Lenin you are, naming your dog Trotsky. Never heard anything so ridiculous, and keep your left-wing politics out of this house.'

'That's it, Amanda, get the kids.'

'But they have just sat down to lunch.'

'I wouldn't eat in the same house as him. We don't want to see you again.'

'My family doesn't want to get together with you, either!'

In their classic book, *Unplug the Christmas Machine*, authors Jo Robinson and Jean Coppock Staeheli say, 'Look at the bounty we are promised by the December magazines and the glowing Christmas commercials: Our families will be together and happy ... We will be truly loved. No wonder we stop, we listen, and we want to believe. The problem comes when we buy into the notion that what we long for can be procured by the buying and selling of goods ... '

The key to unplugging the 'Christmas machine', say the authors, is knowing what you really want. When considering this, you might think about those things, according to child experts, that children really want for Christmas:

- A relaxed and loving time with family
- Realistic expectations about gifts
- An evenly paced season
- Reliable family traditions.

Here are some ways to manage family Christmas stress:

- Find time to ask yourself some questions. How could I create my own family Christmas tradition? Which family members would I like to share this with? Whom do I really want to see, and whom do I feel obliged to see? How do I want or need to spend my time this Christmas? For example, it's a time of the year when many people are tired and run down and need to relax, rather than run frantically round the shops. Which activities do I want to join in, and which ones can be ignored? What did I do last Christmas that didn't work for me?

- Don't get caught up in the family present vendetta. Only buy for those you want to buy for and spend what you can afford. Tell the others that you are opting out of the gift exchange in favour of giving donations to a charity.
- Accept that you are not going to change somebody's beliefs and opinions during one get-together, and that there will be some taboo subjects at family functions.
- Drink in moderation at family gatherings (or not at all). Alcohol tends to magnify emotions and cloud the judgement.
- Try not to respond to what you feel are sub-texts or criticisms from relatives, or to interpret simple statements in a complex way. For example, if someone says, 'It's nice to see you', don't start making assumptions about the rest of the message: 'I haven't actually seen you since last Christmas because you've been too busy with your own life and too selfish to find time, just as you always were.'
- Don't go. If it's really stressful, with a lot of what psychologists call 'dysfunctional acting out' – such as sharp or ambiguous comments, heavy drinking, pointed lateness, or other inconsiderate behaviour – ask yourself if you would put up with this kind of treatment from people who were strangers? Consider taking your main holiday abroad at Christmas, and pay your seasonal visits to parents and close family members before Christmas. People may register annoyance, but why waste your precious time and energy on what could be a special time with your own family and/friends, because other people thrive on emotional chaos?

Family holidays

Expectations of the annual summer holiday are high; with a year's worth of stress to relieve, the pressure to have a good time can be intense. More than 80 per cent of people in the UK become stressed when planning a holiday, according to a survey by NatWest International. The expense of trying to get 'the perfect holiday' is a major factor; trying to avoid crowds is another; and so are the practical considerations such as making arrangements for pets, and packing luggage in line with weight and safety regulations if you are taking a flight.

Another survey from Virgin Holidays found that 34 per cent of parents became so stressed planning a family holiday that they preferred to stay at home, while one in four parents said that holiday planning was more stressful than moving house. As many as two in three families found it difficult to cater for everyone's tastes and expectations when planning a break.

The journey itself can be a source of stress. According to a study by American Express, two-thirds of holidaymakers expect to suffer from some degree of stress before and while on their holiday, with the prospect of delayed flights, crowds and queues coming top of the list.

As with Christmas, one of the problems is that our expectations of holidays are often based on the unrealistic portrayals of healthy, affluent families from television advertisements and travel brochures. The tanned, slim (and often blond) families romping on the beach contrast sadly with the real-life snarling wrecks who eventually arrive at their holiday destination after an exhausting journey. The resulting feelings of failure and inferiority can fuel family stress. So the annual family holidays come high on the stress list, with some justification – especially if you are taking young children abroad, and/or grandparents. There is the stress of the children having too much sun, or stomach upsets, or even the prospect of the annual battle of the towels, with people moving yours – which you so carefully placed to reserve your chosen sun lounger. Holiday stress can start even before you get to the airport. 'Did you lock the back door?' 'Oh no, I left Gran's electric blanket on!' 'Why are you taking so much luggage? I can barely lift it, let alone fit it into the car.'

My own stress highlight – one of them – must have been waiting for a flight around 2 a.m. at Gatwick one year when a series of events led to me wailing, to a distinctly sour-looking member of the airport staff, 'Where is our baby buggy?' I think – though memory has mercifully blotted the details out – that it had got checked in too early, with the rest of the luggage, instead of being handed in at the departure lounge, and we were getting tired lugging our toddler around. Or there was the time when we set out on our return trip from France to the UK at 4 a.m., and managed to drop the wallet containing all the family passports when stopping at a toll. We discovered our loss some 15 kilometres up the motorway, and managed to turn around and head back to the toll where, incredibly, we discovered the wallet, still lying untouched on the ground by the toll booth. The final touch was when, on trying to continue our journey, we were issued with a fine for speeding – such had been our haste to return to look for our missing documentation that we had, apparently, exceeded the time it should have taken us to do the round trip back to the toll!

Every family has similar stories to tell, and though they have their comic aspect afterwards, they are undoubtedly harrowing at the time. Coming back to the realities of life after a holiday can also be stressful – '*Really? That* much? That's a very poor conversion rate' – when the reality of your family holiday spending thuds through your letter box in the form of the credit card statement.

Plan, plan, plan

Consider whether you really want to, or can afford to, go abroad for your holiday. There is a lot of media pressure to take foreign holidays, but exotic holidays can exert a toll in stress and it can sometimes be more restful and recuperative to spend time in the UK. A holiday destination a couple of hours' drive away can work just as well, especially if you have small children.

As these days we have to be conscious of our carbon footprints, a holiday at home can also be an option. If you typically prepare for holidays with a stressful scramble to get all the work and home jobs done before you go, it can be very restful just to wake up in your own bed without the pressure to get up and start enjoying yourself. Holidays at home can be taken at your own pace and you may sometimes benefit more from a chance to be leisurely for a while and enjoy all the activities you always promised yourself – lunches with friends, day trips, visits to the cinema or concerts, shopping. They also offer a chance to catch up on all the undone jobs that have been patiently waiting for you at home – getting them done may relieve you of the stress that stems from a build-up of minor tasks left undone, such as dripping taps, half-decorated rooms, a bare vegetable patch, inadequate storage and so on.

Here are some planning suggestions:

- Different family members want different things from a holiday. Draw up a list of what you would like from your holiday, then a list of what your partner would like. For example, your partner may want the freedom of self-catering, while your dream is to have meals laid on. Be prepared to compromise; can you go self-catering but go out for some meals?
- Draw up another list detailing the needs of any children. Most small children don't really appreciate the cultural subtleties of foreign

travel, but are happy with safe space, and opportunities for exercise such as a swimming pool, sea, sand, bicycles, and trees to climb. Do you have to go abroad? For older children and teenagers, activity holidays such as skiing and walking may be more appropriate.

- Don't leave everything until the last minute – this is the best way to build stress levels. Once you know where you want to go, book it. It is a myth that leaving it to the last minute automatically means a bargain. Do also allow plenty of time for any holiday purchases.
- Check out your destination at the Foreign and Commonwealth Office website (<www.fco.gov.uk>). The 'Know Before You Go' part of the site gives valuable information on dos and don'ts you should be aware of.
- Try to ensure you leave at a comfortable time – not too early, not too late. Night-time travel may seem like a good idea at the time, but a night's lost sleep can cost you two days to recover and sets the scene for a truly stressful holiday.
- Travel light – don't pack more than you really need. You can always buy at your destination.
- Make sure laptops and, if possible, mobile phones are left behind, so you're not tempted to check work e-mails. Nearly half of all Britons worry about work while on holiday – an ideal recipe for stress.
- Once there, give yourself time to unwind. It takes most people three to four days to lose thoughts of work and home, which is why the traditional two-week break once a year is a good idea. However, do also look at the tips for shorter breaks in the section on 'weekends' below.

Weekend stress

Weekends should ideally be a retreat from the world. Unfortunately, some people overdo the unwinding process, and evidence of weekend stress is all too clearly shown by weekend police reports and records of hospital emergency visits.

Most families lead busy lives, and weekends, which used to be a time for resting and spending time as a family, are now packed even more full – activities and hobbies for children, shopping and other errands.

The valuable spare time, so vital for recharging, can also become a battleground. What are we doing this weekend? 'Let's go and visit Gran,' cry the kids. But Michael and his family will be there. Already the stress factor has risen. Torn between the children's desire to see their grandmother and the doubt about being around the provocative

Michael, the husband and wife argue about the merits of the visit versus the boredom of hanging round at home for yet another weekend.

Finally, they decide to do nothing and flop around all weekend watching television. Gran has the last word: 'I'm glad you didn't come this weekend, darling. Michael's girls were appalled at the suggested gathering, so it is probably better you didn't come along.'

'Oh really, Mother.' Wife puts the phone down. 'Right, that does it. We are never seeing them again.'

So take the pressure off. A quiet weekend can be a real de-stressor. Don't feel you have to schedule anything for the weekend. Keep it free, and see what you feel like doing. One outing a day, or even one outing per weekend, may be enough.

Sometimes you can spend more money by hanging around at home for the weekend than you would on an economical weekend away, so why not plan a long weekend away? Pick a destination within an hour's drive or flight to minimize the stress of travel and to ensure that you spend the maximum amount of time actually enjoying the break.

9

Building trust and acknowledgement

A good family story would be one in which important needs, wishes, feelings and beliefs of family members become more acknowledged by one another. For many families, this is the case. Their home is a warm and intimate retreat where they can come in and relax, a stress-free zone. However, for many the home is too often the site of significant interpersonal and social stress. Tearing at their hair, metaphorically or otherwise, many family members cry out, 'How is it that our family can come to this? Why are we communicating like this?'

Communication is paramount if you are to reap the benefits of close family relationships. That means taking responsibility for our own actions. So it is never productive, and rarely accurate, to identify our problem as someone else's behaviour (another member of the family). More accurately, our problem is how we are affected by the other person's behaviour. So how do we approach a stress-causing family conflict, which on the face of it looks intractable?

Dialogue

Well, one way is to sit down and talk it out rationally.

Talking, or dialogue, is important for many reasons. One key aspect is that dialogue helps us to weed out errors. We gain an opportunity to correct our own mistakes when we attend and respond to objections offered by another person with a perspective different from our own. In this way, dialogue can contribute to accuracy. The merging of one perspective with another may provide new possibilities; a new idea may stimulate a novel thought which in turn provokes another thought. In such cases, the whole can be greater than the sum of its parts. In this way, through dialogue and acknowledgement, we foster trust. Of course, in such a family dialogue you must be prepared to be open. To be open you must trust the person you are talking to.

Trust and dialogue

The conventional family starts out with vows of trust (marriage). You trust the implications of what the other says, that he or she will give you the full extent of their love, time, effort, money and other resources. This union is only worth risking if 'I trust you'.

Genuine family dialogue presupposes trust. For such dialogue, members of a family need to sincerely express themselves, make reliable claims, then interpret one another's claims carefully. They must listen attentively, hearing one another's reasons and arguments, and being sensitive to the other's feelings and values. This reciprocity is essential to a 'genuine dialogue'.

This suggests that there are many non-genuine dialogues. We may want to talk but not listen, and even when we seem to be listening, we may be waiting with suppressed impatience for our own chance to speak. Even when we do listen attentively, we too often simply disagree or agree, failing to respond actively to the reasons and sentiments of the other person. We may just record his or her ideas as some kind of given without responding intellectually or emotionally. Another failure of response is trying to manipulate the other person into saying what we want.

When one person distrusts another, it affects his interpretation of his actions, 'Yes, you can borrow my bicycle. But would you mind leaving me a deposit?' This is hardly relying on the good disposition of the other. 'Keep your bike, then,' can be the expected response.

In non-diagnostic listening, we listen without interrupting and we suppress the need to get our penny-worth in; instead we engage in active listening. Indicating that one 'hears' the other is central to this – for example, by briefly repeating back to the person what he or she has just said. Obviously interrupting and name-calling should be avoided; I think you'd agree that this essentially counts as *non*-acknowledgement.

How distrust disables us

Once distrust is established in a family it can be difficult to overcome. If we distrust someone, we feel uneasy in his or her presence; we feel vulnerable, and we are likely to try to protect ourselves by holding back. Distrust disables us from being able to believe what this family member says. We may suspect the person of deception in many forms: biasing his/her information, omitting relevant points, failing to acknowledge obvious objections to his/her own position, and even outright lying, in an attempt to manipulate us or exploit our willingness to listen and communicate. We may be so sensitive to potential affronts or threats that we may make allegations on the basis of insufficient evidence. Even accurate and well-intentioned messages may be misinterpreted.

The energy put into distrust of family members is stress-inducing in itself.

The 'confirmation fallacy'

Distrust has a powerful tendency to grow in self-fulfilling spirals. In the 'confirmation fallacy', we seek evidence to support what we already believe – 'I know she is like that, and her latest behaviour is consistent with my belief.' We tend to ignore other evidence: 'But she was trying to be honest this time round, she really has turned over a new leaf.' There is a tendency in us not to accept anything that disproves our favoured hypotheses: 'She's not to be trusted, and that's that!'

Rebuilding trust

How, though, do we rebuild trust if someone in the family has behaved badly and broken that trust? The connection between acknowledgement and trust can be readily appreciated when you are trying to become reconciled after one family member has wronged another. If, as is all too often the case, a wrongdoer is unwilling to acknowledge that he has done wrong, the wronged person has no basis for assurance that such things will not be repeated.

Acknowledgement and apology

There may be two kinds of apologies in family conflict: those that express remorse and those that express regret. It is important to keep them separate yet recognize the importance of both.

Remorse is the pure apology, in which someone expresses sorrow at an action done. In this case, someone says, 'If I had the chance again, I just wouldn't do that.' Remorse offers a future for the relationship.

The second kind of apology expresses regret and is sometimes called a 'pseudo apology'. In this case, someone regrets the harm he or she has done to another, but, if given the chance again, would have still acted in the same way. This kind of apology can sometimes have the effect of sweeping everything under the carpet. This is useful if you just need to get on with life for a while; all families just go through the motions sometimes. But it may also signal the need to evaluate things a little more than that. You may have to limit your expectations of a person who indulges in this kind of apology.

Interestingly, remorse as a mitigating factor plays an important part in law. Juries who witness the defendant showing what seems to be *genuine* remorse will look more kindly on the accused.

Regret is concerned with good versus bad consequences; remorse is concerned with right versus wrong action.

This leads us on to trying to judge the 'sincerity' of an apology. Time is really the best arbitrator of that, however. All you can do is give the other person a chance – if you want to.

When trust and acknowledgement have really broken down

Dealing with the difficult family member

- You can make a fundamental decision to cut off all emotional energy from the troublesome family member. Stop wearing yourself out. It's your energy. Put yourself first and treat yourself the way you want other family members to treat you.
- Focus on those family members with whom you do feel comfortable – perhaps the quieter ones who stay in the background, away from the family shenanigans. An ally can be worth his or her weight in gold at the next difficult family gathering.
- Ask the troublesome family member if he or she would like to discuss the situation, at a time when the whole family isn't together. *If* the other person seems receptive, stay calm and start by listening to what he or she has to say. This in itself is often a great healer.
- Without blaming yourself or the other person for what has happened, offer your apologies for where you yourself may have gone wrong in the past, and show where you may have misunderstood the other or behaved in a way you would change if you could. Hopefully the other person will be able to do the same.
- Set limits – for example, how often you are prepared to see the troublesome member, what you are prepared to put up with, and what you need from him or her, such as honesty, openness or respect, if the relationship is to continue. 'Kind but firm' is the word here. Take charge and state your needs without falling back into frustration, getting into a power struggle, or letting the other treat you like a doormat.
- If the other person is not receptive, or if such a meeting is unlikely, it's probably better just to let it go. Try to forgive the other person – this doesn't mean grand emotional gestures and reconciliations; it just means letting go of your feelings of resentment and anger. You can forgive and not see that person again if you wish.
- Be realistic. Don't expect your stubborn, insensitive, self-absorbed relative to metamorphose into Mother Teresa. Family therapist and

author Dr Leonard Felder recommends that you set a realistic small goal that will allow you to feel successful. For example, if a ten-minute phone call or a two-hour visit is the most you can handle with a particularly difficult relative, don't volunteer for an hour-long phone call or a seven-day visit that is bound to turn out badly. Meanwhile, the key thing is not to harm yourself by harbouring resentment.

- Change your goals. Instead of trying to change the other person, just concentrate on getting through meetings feeling relaxed. Keep such meetings brief and polite. You don't have to be best friends just because you're family, and you can keep in touch without having every Sunday lunch or Christmas together.
- You choose the venue when you get together. Instead of meeting at home, with all its associations, arrange to meet in public – a shop, a café, an art gallery – or go for a walk. Find something you might both enjoy.
- Accept the reality – don't whitewash the situation. This is an important part of accepting the other person for what he or she is. Don't ask your unreliable sister to come for Boxing Day if you know her car is going to 'break down', don't phone your grandmother for a heart-to-heart about your problematic love affair if you know she's only interested in regurgitating old stories about her own dysfunctional marriage. Get your needs met by other, more reliable people.
- Use humour. Robert nicknamed his particularly difficult 17-year-old daughter Cruella de Vil. The name caught on like wildfire throughout the family, who were relieved to have found a humorous way of dealing with this prickly adolescent.

Coping with rude, patronizing relatives

- Accept and deflect. Say, 'That's very interesting. I hear you're thinking of moving house/have got promotion.' In other words, don't react, and change the subject.
- Calmly set limits. Say, 'I don't think you've got that quite right' or 'I'd rather you didn't talk to me in that way.'
- Walk away.

Dealing with the truly toxic family member

Misunderstandings and lack of communication are one thing: the family member who's more grumpy, critical or demanding than average; our mother who loves us, but still thinks she knows best; or the unthinking, insensitive, selfish member who makes our blood boil but whom we really do love deep down. But someone who is really emotionally toxic is different. It might be the person whose cutting comments you always dread at meetings, or whose drinking makes any situation go out of control. You may be dealing with someone who has a personality disorder, is disturbed, or who harbours real hatred or just doesn't care.

Old wounds often underlie this kind of person's behaviour and attitude. Other family members may be able to tell you when and how this extra-difficult family member changed from being a kind soul into an angry or self-absorbed person. Phillip, for example, was thought to have changed after a spell in the army; and Jonathan, who ballooned to double his weight, became hard and distant after a year as a foreign exchange trader in the City.

More understanding of a wounded soul does not, however, mean you have to accommodate the toxic comments and personality traits, or to pretend the problem doesn't exist, or to whitewash or laugh off the hurtful things he or she says or does. It puts the matter in context as the other person's problem, one that has nothing to do with you. It may also clarify when there is a situation of no hope.

This is obviously the option of last resort, but if you can see the relationship is just not going to work, if there's been a long-term problem that is likely to continue, if the person shows no remorse, then sometimes you have no option but to distance yourself or say goodbye in order to protect yourself and perhaps your own immediate family.

Acknowledgement and non-acknowledgement

Acknowledgement is a mediating tool and plays a key part in family conflict resolution.

There are different kinds of non-acknowledgement. In a dialogue, we may not acknowledge what another family member is saying by ignoring his or her contributions, by asking questions and failing to wait for the answer, by interrupting, by stereotyping, discounting or denigrating the person or, worse still, by insulting or seeking to humiliate him or her. Also, non-acknowledgement need not be conveyed in words: it can be expressed in gestures or actions.

William

William was an eminent doctor who had emigrated from his native UK to the USA. There he was much respected and had many friends. When he returned to the UK, though, he always felt that it was he who made all the enquiries with the other adult members in his family, while he waited patiently and in vain for reciprocal interest. Any moment now, he used to think, my brother (or sister) I am talking to will ask me a question. But after the routine, 'All well with you then?', there was, William felt, a complete lack of curiosity from his family. This was even more infuriating to William than it might have been to some people as curiosity was really at the heart of his life – without curiosity, or a fascinated interest in others, he felt he wouldn't have become a doctor. William couldn't understand how the people 'from whom he had come' could be so dull. It wasn't that he wanted to boast about his success – just to share his new life a bit.

William had evidently forgotten the old wisdom that 'a prophet is respected everywhere but in his own country'. In fact, William was well on the way to making an 'alternative family' in the USA. He already had a circle of working colleagues who shared his research interests and were very interested in his work. He was developing true friends as well; and later he married an American woman, acquiring her relations in the process, whom he found much more sympathetic than his own. 'Everyone likes to talk about themselves, but at least I found people who do listen, and who are both attentive and curious about others,' said William. (See Chapter 10 for more on alternative families.)

In a genuine family dialogue, the 'otherness' of the other person is taken seriously and regarded as an opportunity, not an obstacle. In an ideal world, the father may say to his wayward daughter, Alice, 'I will not impose my will on you.' To acknowledge the other is to admit, and indicate in gestures and words, that our own perspectives are not the only ones relevant to the discussion. We have no entitlement to the last word.

'Regression' in the family situation

One problem with long-term conflict in a family is that of 'regression' – it can pull you back to an earlier state of being or a previous stage of life. It is quite common to find that family members regress to earlier behaviour patterns at family gatherings. If, for example, you were always seen as the rebel, you may find you're almost unwittingly refusing food and drinks, making contrary replies to comments, and generally acting in a rather more aggressive way than has come to be usual these days. Conversely, if you were the goody-goody, you may revert to not being able to say boo to a goose! If you've grown out of old roles and they no longer reflect who you are, it can be stressful to feel pulled towards them again. It can be stressful for partners, too.

Alan

Alan's family were highly combative and competitive and had had more quarrels than he could count over the years. Alan himself naturally preferred a quieter style, but, when meeting family, would get enraged at members who, he felt, saw him as insignificant and not worthy of respect. He felt he was invisible or, at best, patronized at family meetings. 'I was wallpaper and, worse, not only did they not talk to me, they ignored my teenage children too, who were incredibly hurt. No matter what I may have achieved in the outside world – which they showed not a jot of interest in – when I saw my family, I was always just "the little brother" – the disregarded youngest. Well, I will show them.'

But as the years rolled on, he didn't show them; every time he met his family, the old feelings of rage and resentment would surface, not allowing room for him to show the new person he felt he had become away from his family.

This was not really a case of looking for opportunities to mend relationships. The family as a whole was too large, unruly and aggressive, too much harm had been done in the past, and Alan's style was too different from theirs. He was, frankly, banging his head against a brick wall trying to get their attention and respect. He was separate from the clan.

However, if this is a problem for you, but your family aren't beyond hope, try the following:

- When you next meet with your family, try – without being aggressive – to express an opinion or two that may not match how you used to think.
- Also, try seeing your family members as they are now, instead of letting their previous roles dominate your viewpoint.
- Stay away from old bones of contention and go armed with a list of subjects to discuss, such as current affairs, interesting scientific discoveries, and so on.
- Try to meet family on their own territory. For example, if your father's hobby is gardening, steam railways or the stock market, why not read up a little about it before the next meeting?

Sibling rivalry

Rejection, or perceived rejection, by the clan is different from sibling rivalry, though the two may overlap. Sibling rivalry seems to have a particular grip on the imagination today and is rarely mentioned without a throwaway reference to Cain and Abel; perhaps it's a reflection on our competitive culture.

Laura

At the age of 44, Laura decided on a 'clean slate' with her sister – no more rows, no more recriminations – for the sake of their respective children. (Each had three children around the same age.) It was approximately after two years of 'making an effort' that Laura realized that, no matter how hard she tried to behave – doing all the right things, making the first move, being willing to forget the past, and so on – things were just not going to work. Her sister was genuinely uninterested. 'I realized it had nothing to do with me,' said Laura. 'That's just the way things were.'

Seeing things as they were, and not as she wanted them to be, was a painful process for Laura, not so much for her own sake as for what she wanted for her children. 'I had to let go of a whole image of cousins together, building up relationships and family memories through sleep-overs and weekends and holidays together.' Her sister had her own friends; she socialized with these peers and encouraged her children to form bonds with their children, and showed almost no interest in Laura's children.

Opinions on sibling rivalry vary, with some psychologists taking a more positive view and others a more negative one. Some see it as a natural animal instinct where young ones tussle for attention in order to survive, like puppies. Others view it as a healthy part of sibling life, teaching children how to resolve conflict and accept the integral unfairness of life.

Those such as Dr Deborah Gold, assistant professor of psychiatry and sociology at Duke University, and Dr Stephen Bank, professor of psychology at Wesleyan University, feel that rivalry is not a necessary state of affairs, and that getting on well with our siblings is a 'birthright'.

Others, such as Judy Dunn, are less accommodating of the 'birthright' factor, taking the view that innate personality clashes, along with the tremendous competition for parents' love and attention, can make living cheek by jowl together for years very hard for some siblings. Dunn's studies of young children show that as young as one year, siblings are sensitive to differences of treatment by parents in relation to their siblings.

Sibling relationships are, however, generally agreed to be fluid and subtle, and can change over the years. Dunn found that events such as a mother's illness or death made siblings much more supportive. Likewise, key events in adulthood can have an effect on sibling relationships, especially the death of a parent, getting married, and starting your own family. Ageing can also sometimes make siblings closer – once parents have died, and brothers and sisters face their own mortality, sibling bonds can become stronger.

It's been estimated that a third of us continue to have conflict with our siblings into adulthood. Whether this is set in stone or not, it's surprisingly common for siblings to feel that a parent is closer to, or more supportive of, one adult child than another:

'Jane was always Dad's favourite, and now he visits her every weekend for tea. Doesn't it ever occur to him to come and see us too?'

'Mum pays her duty visits to see the children, but her heart is really with my sister. She spends far more time with them – weekends and Christmas are invariably spent with her. She just naturally feels more comfortable with my sister and her values, which are different to mine.'

'My brother always takes my father's side in an argument. In fact, there never is any argument; his eyes glaze over and the subject is changed. You can't get through to him. It drives me mad!'

The acuteness of a young child to differences in treatment persists into adulthood. But, while babies' social awareness is far more sophisticated than was once imagined, they can't yet understand why they may be being treated differently. Many adult siblings aren't able to see the total picture, either.

There are reasons why parents might spend more time with one adult child than the others: geography – one child lives closest to her parents; or shared personality traits or values. It's easy to interpret this as meaning that a parent 'loves' the other sibling more, whereas they just feel closer or more invested in their lives, for whatever reason. Continuing to compete only sets the scene for more hurt and misunderstanding. It's better to accept the relationships for what they are – as well as what they are not.

It is OK to accept that you may not get as much support, interest and approval from parents and siblings as you want. Instead, if you have a family of your own, or a partner, why not focus on creating what you would have liked to have had from your family of origin. That they couldn't provide it is really their problem – a family or relationship of your own provides a wonderful new chance to re-create things as you would have liked them to be.

Ubunto

The importance of acknowledging people, of respecting them and attending to their perspective, is elegantly captured in the African notion of *ubuntu*, which expresses a notion of persons as essentially relational and existing through their connections with other people. Archbishop Desmond Tutu explained the notion of *ubuntu* as follows: '*Ubuntu* is very difficult to render into a Western language. It speaks of the very essence of being human. When we want to give high praise to someone we say, "Yu, u no *ubuntu*", "Hey, so-and-so has *ubuntu*". Then you are generous, you are hospitable, you are friendly and caring and compassionate. You share what you have to say, "My humanity is caught up, is inextricably bound up, in yours." We belong in a bundle of life. We say, "A person is a person through other persons." Here the Cartesian knot is lovingly unsnarled; it is not the Cartesian, "I think therefore I am." It is rather: "I am because I belong. I participate, I share, therefore I exist."' This sentiment is endorsed by Harvard scientist Edward Osborne Wilson: 'I link therefore I exist.'

10

The power of the group

During the Second World War in London, Anna Freud studied children under stress from continued bombing. Out of this she coined the word 'coping'. Sometimes it may not be possible to change situations outright, but it is possible to cope with them, and this chapter looks at one of the most effective and well-documented ways of doing just that: using your social support.

Building your resiliency

The mountain flowers called columbines thrive on their ability to weather extreme cold. They grow and bloom profusely at the opportune moment, season after season, making the most of their hostile environment. Columbines are resilient.

Equally, the capacity for physical, psychological and spiritual resiliency renewal and recovery, in the face of stress or trauma, is currently receiving much academic and medical research. From studies of children who thrive under adversity, family researchers have applied the concept of resilience to family adaptation.

Understanding and interpreting these insights is a critical role of family-life educators. We are not talking of a kind of James Bond '007' bounce-back elasticity here, but a resilience which is a process of adapting well in the face of stress, be it adversity or even trauma.

As mentioned earlier, a network of supportive relationships has been identified as one of the key factors in fending off family stress. That it helps stress in general is also well-established. According to Sir Michael Marmot, professor of epidemiology and public health at University College London, there are more than ten long-term studies that show that good social support leads to a lower risk of death. Good relationships are also key to longevity, and help stave off depression, as well as boosting the development of the brain and immune system.

One Australian study even pinpointed friends, not family, as being the key to a longer life. Previous research had not distinguished between social contact with friends or relatives. This study of 1,500 70-year-olds found that people who reported regular close contact with five or more friends were 22 per cent less likely to die in the next decade than those who had reported fewer, more-distant friends. But the presence or absence of close ties with relatives had no impact on survival. Friends are perhaps less likely to be a source of negative stress than family can sometimes be, concluded researchers at Flinders University in Adelaide.

We can only expect so much from our families. At their best, they provide a unique type of social support. They may give emotional and practical support in times of crisis, sometimes even financial support to tide us over when we're desperate. Our families carry our history: no one else can talk over childhood memories, help us re-live those early and most powerful experiences, or remember parts of ourselves we've forgotten or didn't even know about. At its best, the family offers a special refuge from stress. In adult life, however, it's unrealistic to ask family for what they cannot provide.

In the interests of mature companionship, it may be worthwhile trying to extend your family – that is, to cultivate warm, close friends who can act as family and perhaps give you what your own family is unable to provide.

'Extended' families/your 'true' family

For some people, their family of origin is not their 'true family', and they eventually have to accept that they have not been born into families who think like them and share their values. There are, however, many people in the world with whom they may have more in common, and who may be able to provide the support, love and acceptance that isn't forthcoming from their family members.

This kind of 'true family' or 'extended family' comes in different forms: friends, partners, in-laws, people met at activities or support groups. These days, a truly enthralling hobby can mean you become enrolled in a global family. Jill, for example, collected vintage children's books and found her contact with other collectors just as much fun as the books themselves. For some, work provides an extended family.

The secret is to seek out people who are able to meet your needs. Confide a personal disaster to a trustworthy friend, rather than to a disinterested sister; discuss work problems with a respected peer, rather than brothers who are too immersed in the family business to listen. This helps both you and your family by releasing them from pressure and unrealistic expectations, so removing a source of conflict.

'Social capital'

Sadly, when trying to cope with the effects of family tension, outside relationships are often neglected. Isolating oneself can be a natural response to family problems – you just don't want to talk about them, or to expose yourself to the advice or feedback of others.

In his seminal book *Bowling Alone: The Collapse and Revival of American Community*, Robert Putnam, a professor of sociology at Harvard University, looks in depth at the value of social networks, and voices his alarm that these are declining. Putnam coined the phrase 'social capital', which might be loosely defined as social trust in practice. Putnam argues that American civic society is breaking down – or, as he puts it, 'the bonds of our communities have withered' – as people have increasingly less contact with friends, neighbours and the community. Even sociable Sunday picnics are in decline, he finds.

A variety of quite specific benefits flow from the trust, reciprocity, information and co-operation associated with social networks. Social capital creates value for the people who are connected and – at least sometimes – for bystanders as well. Despite the capitalist metaphor (even social contact is viewed as a commodity, and Putnam reports that getting married is the equivalent of quadrupling your income, while attending a club meeting regularly is the equivalent of doubling your income), the book does make the point that, even at the most selfish level, social contact is good for us as well as for others.

Ways of assessing your 'social capital' vary a great deal, but the list below offers a starting point in thinking about its role in your life:

- I spend a lot of time visiting friends.
- I agree that most people are honest and can be 'trusted'.
- I have attended at least one public meeting on community affairs in the last year.
- I have been to at least one club meeting in the last year.
- I have one or more group memberships.
- I have volunteered once or more in the last year.
- I entertain once or more a month.
- I meet friends for lunch or a drink at least once a month.
- I have become involved with a community project in the last year.
- I have served on the committee of a local organization in the last year.

Sociability starts with the family

How often do you do the following things together as a family unit:

- Have the main meal together?
- Sit and talk together?
- Watch television together?
- Go out to eat together?
- Take a holiday together?
- Attend religious services together?
- Exercise/play sports together?

These things are worth thinking about. They are activities that we maybe think we do, but that, on consideration, often get swept away in the pressures of daily living. Try monitoring how much time you spend as a family on the above in an average week.

If you haven't already tried them, here are some more social activities to try as a family:

- Read a favourite book together.
- Look at old photos.
- Fly a kite.
- Buy a badminton or table tennis set.
- Take a family bicycle ride.
- Visit museums, art galleries or historical sites together.
- Have that picnic!

Expanding your social network

It can take courage and a few risks to make friends or strengthen existing ties. There are many potential meeting places – evening classes, community projects, support groups, local health clubs, volunteer activities, etc. It's also worth putting more effort into maintaining old tried and trusted friendships (and conversely spending less time and energy on unprofitable family members).

For more suggestions, see *Overcoming Loneliness and Making Friends*, by Márianna Csóti (Sheldon Press 2005).

The spiritual dimension

Nearly one thousand studies have indicated that those who go to a place of worship are healthier than their 'faithless' counterparts – and live an average seven years longer. One in ten of the nuns of the convent of the School Sisters of Notre Dame in Minnesota have managed to reach their 100th birthday. No matter what your beliefs are, however, experts believe that a sense of community, and of belief in something larger than yourself, are vital ingredients in a long and happy life.

11

Re-defining your family

Studies show that the personality traits of optimism and pessimism can affect how well you live and even how long you live. It is possible to reduce stress by changing negative thoughts to positive.

The endless stream of thoughts that run through your head every day may be positive or negative. Some comes from logic and reason; some comes from misconceptions, lack of information and distorted ideas.

Some common forms of irrational thinking are:

- *Filtering.* You magnify the negative aspects of a situation and filter out all the positive ones. For example, it has been a very busy day and a happy one with the family. But you overlooked one thing – you forgot to ask Carmel about her money situation and now she has gone back to university. That evening, you focus only on your oversight and forget about the compliments you received.
- *Personalizing.* When something bad occurs, you automatically blame yourself. For example, Anna's father is unwell; she has heard this through someone who is not a member of her family. She feels insulted that none of her family have told her, and assumes it's her fault that none of her family wants to know her.
- *Catastrophizing.* You automatically anticipate the worst. Ian is going to London and he automatically fears it is going to be a disaster. Or you envisage one change in your daily routine as being a disaster for your whole day.
- *Polarizing.* You see things only as either good or bad. There is no middle ground. You feel that you have to be perfect or you're a total failure.

With time and practice, it is possible to turn negative thoughts into positive ones, and this is the idea behind the most popular and effective type of therapy, cognitive behavioural therapy.

Examples of typical negative thinking and how you might apply a positive twist are shown in Table 1:

Table 1 Negative thinking and positive thinking

Negative thinking	Positive thinking
I've never tried this approach with the family.	It's an opportunity to learn something new.
It's all too complicated with the family.	I can view it from a different angle.
I don't have the resources to deal with the family.	But I have to live with them, so why don't I try?
There's not enough time to deal with family and their issues.	Maybe I should evaluate some of my priorities.
There's no way it will work with my family.	At least I can try to make it work.
I don't have the expertise to deal with such family problems.	I'll find people who can help me.
I have done enough for the family.	There's always room for improvement.
It's too radical a change to try this with them.	Let's take a chance.
No one in this family bothers to communicate with me.	I'll see if I can open the channels of communication.
I'm not going to get any better at dealing with their problems.	I'll give it one more try.
I'm never going to learn how to manage my stress.	I'm going to try to learn how to manage my stress.

Practical tips

- If you are having difficulty in understanding a problem, try drawing a picture of it. Include family members.
- If you just can't find a solution, try assuming that you have a solution and seeing what you can derive from that ('working backwards').
- For one week, act as if you had solved the problem. Then re-examine it.
- Turn your attention to a smaller, more practical problem initially, such as always having to rush for work in the morning, and build up your confidence by working on that first.

Family therapy

Family therapy, as the name implies, focuses on understanding psychological difficulties in the context of social relationships, and would view a problem within the context of the family as a whole, rather than focusing on a single person. While it often takes place when there is a problem with a child, it can take place with only adults present.

It evaluates the relationships, ideas and attitudes of all the family and, once these are clear, the therapist may work with the family to try to get it to see its position more objectively and clearly, and for members to behave or relate to one another in different ways.

Family therapy is usually recommended by a health professional such as a doctor, or sometimes you can go directly to a specialist centre.

Cognitive behavioural therapy (CBT)

Cognitive behavioural therapy (CBT) is one of the so-called 'talking therapies' well known for being effective for many disorders such as anxiety and stress in family situations. Unfortunately, it can be difficult to access through the NHS, and you may have to wait if you want to get CBT without paying for it. Private therapy is another option, but you need to ensure that therapists are properly qualified; ask your doctor, or check with a professional body for a list of accredited practitioners, such as the British Association for Behavioural and Cognitive Psychotherapies (see Useful addresses at the end of this book).

In CBT, the focus is on finding the negative thoughts that cause stress and anxiety, and then looking for the deeply held underlying assumptions that lead to these harmful thinking patterns. It's based on the idea that how we think (cognition), how we feel (emotion) and how we act (behaviour) all interact together. Our thoughts determine our feelings and our behaviour. Therefore, negative and unrealistic thoughts can cause stress and result in problems.

A typical negative thought leading to stress would be: 'I'm just not going to be able to look after my ageing mother properly/fulfil the demands of the family business'. The underlying assumption might be: 'I've never been any good and my family have always known it' or 'I have to work harder than most people to gain my family's approval' or 'Now my family will really find me out'.

Naturally, such thoughts and assumptions have a terrific negative impact on mood, causing feelings of depression and inadequacy, especially if, as often happens, you don't quite realize where they're coming from or what's going on. The problem may be worsened if you also react by avoiding situations and activities likely to arouse anxiety. In this case, a successful experience becomes more unlikely, which re-inforces the original thought of 'I've never been any good' – and so we have a self-fulfilling prophecy.

Such repetitive thinking is addressed in CBT by developing more flexible thought patterns. CBT does not try to teach people to view things more positively, but more realistically. Under stress, someone often sees situations in a distorted manner. For instance, you might think that something awful has happened to one of your family every time the phone rings (even though, time and again, this is not the case). In those seconds before you pick up the phone, you may already have run the gamut of immediate stress reactions such as quickened heartbeat, shallow breathing and clammy hands.

CBT suggests you keep a diary to record negative thoughts, and see how these affect stress and anxiety. The aim is to recognize when and under which circumstances such negative thoughts start, and ultim-ately to view stressors differently and to think and react in a new way. For example, you could just try suspending your judgement until you pick up the phone.

It differs from psychodynamic therapy, or the traditional analytic type of therapy that tends to look more into the individual's uncon-scious or subconscious mind to get at the 'truth' of what is going on. Much psychodynamic therapy places the onus fairly and squarely on the client; this is often the typical long-term Freudian therapy of long silences and an unforthcoming therapist. It's rather out of fashion (and expensive) these days.

Negative thoughts, which may lead to stress and depression, are generally about one or more of three areas:

- Negative view of self
- Negative view of the world
- Negative view of the future.

These constitute what Aaron Beck, the father of cognitive therapy, called the 'cognitive triad'.

The ABC of irrational beliefs

A major aid in CBT is what Albert Ellis called the ABC Technique of Irrational Beliefs, to help analyse the process by which you may develop irrational beliefs. Ellis developed a form of CBT called rational emotive behaviour therapy (REBT) in 1955, and the ABC forms a tool in this. When Ellis presented his first paper on REBT at the 1956

American Psychological Association Annual Convention, he listed 12 common irrational beliefs. He went on to list over fifty common irrational beliefs, but has since realized that there are scores of irrational beliefs that people can hold! This is an exercise you might like to try, based on this:

A. Activating event or situation

Record an event or circumstance that makes you feel frustrated and upset. For example, having to go to your mother's for lunch, or phoning your brother, who doesn't let you get a word in edgeways.

B. Beliefs

Write down the negative thoughts that result from this. For example, 'I can't stand wasting my Sunday going to this lunch; my mother is absolutely wrong to make me; my brother must listen to me.'

C. Consequences

Now specify the negative feelings that result – for example, frustration, self-dislike, anger.

We then go on to:

D. Disputing the irrational belief

This means asking questions to test whether the belief is realistic, logical and, ultimately, whether it helps achieve goals or if it only leads to more misery. For example, 'Do I actually have to go to this lunch?', 'Is anybody really making me go?' or 'Who says my brother has to listen to me? Can he in fact choose not to listen to me?'

E. Enacting an effective new, more rational belief to replace the previous belief which had no real grounding in reason

For example, 'I do not have to go to lunch and maybe instead I will choose to make a briefer visit around teatime; this would also be helpful to my mother who finds the lighter meal easier to prepare.' Or, 'I do not have to make my brother see my point of view or take in what I say. I can find someone else to talk to.'

CBT may be particularly useful when family is the problem as it can help tackle thought patterns learned at an early age, especially if you've always been taught to expect the worst. For example, it can help to change unrealistic assumptions such as that it's always your duty to put things right with family members, or that other family members' moods have been caused by your wrongdoing, or that whatever goes wrong in family is always your fault. If you have a habit of thinking such negative thoughts, you will suffer from stress, and find awkward family members stressful, whatever you do. This isn't a question of blaming yourself – far from it. But it does mean you need to re-learn certain thinking patterns until you start to think realistically, to minimize situations of family stress.

Once you have identified thinking errors, you will be able immediately to identify when your thinking is drifting, and be able to take instant action to change this.

Computerized CBT

Computerized CBT (CCBT) is not a replacement for face-to-face therapy, but can provide an option, especially given the lack of available therapists in the UK. It is probably more suitable for individuals than families, especially those who prefer to take charge of a problem themselves and don't feel comfortable sitting talking to a therapist. CCBT for anxiety and mild depression is available in some NHS practices. Consult your GP for more detail.

Defining and re-inventing your family

In Chapter 3, we looked at the importance of family 'myths' and stories. This focused on the type of story-with-a-grain-of-truth we are all so familiar with – for example, John is the success, Jane is the black sheep.

A variation on this is the family story about our ancestors. Colourful figures in the family past hold a special place in family stories, often akin to what happens in the party game of Chinese whispers. Over time, their role becomes distorted and exaggerated. Again, there is probably a grain of truth in such stories, but the heroic stature ascribed to some ancestors may be more doubtful.

Sometimes too other aspects of the family become dramatized over time, such as health, and it can be important to sort out the facts. A reliable family history can literally be a life-saver. Does breast cancer or heart disease run in the family? If so, are you a candidate for early screening or other preventative measures? If secrecy is the 'story' in your family, is now the time to be asking older relatives some hard questions about the true nature of the family health?

Karen and Sara

Karen's younger sister, Sara, was convinced that their mother had died of bowel cancer and, in later life, started booking herself in for extensive bowel cancer screening. Karen did her best to explain that the cancer had in fact started as breast cancer, and spread to the bowel along with the rest of the body in the very last stages of the illness. Sara obstinately refused to listen and persisted with the frequent screening for some years until the medical specialists themselves gently suggested it be done less frequently.

Linked to this is the question of having children. Genetic counselling may be important to dispel myths about illness in the family. Sociologist of medicine Dr Katie Featherstone, at the University of Cardiff, has written of how information about genetic disease isn't always passed on 'straight' through the family; the family dynamics of passing on or withholding information and medical options can be complex. If you know or suspect there may be genetic disease in the family, try and get it straight, both with family members and with your doctor, who should be able to refer you for genetic counselling.

Clarifying the famous family legend

Whether it's to do with genetic disease, or the fact that one of your ancestors rowed the boat for Bonnie Prince Charlie, at some point you may want to find some evidence to support the family story:

1 Make a record of the family story. Ask several relatives to relate it to you and note it down in detail or record it. Ask about any points that are unclear.

2 Ask where they heard the story to see if they heard it from different sources.

3 Once you have a few versions of the story, study the detail and look for similarities and discrepancies. Similarities may be indicators of the truth of the facts. The inconsistencies may be less likely to be rooted in fact.

4 Ask for back-up, such as letters, photos, press cuttings and so on.

5 Start formal research if you want. Researching your family tree is enormously popular, and a sign of how important our origins are to us. Genealogy itself is rather beyond the scope of this book, but if you want more information, your local library may well be able to help you get started, or try the web pages given in the box below.

Genealogy

If this is a subject that you find interesting, you will find the following websites useful:

The Federation of Family History Societies (FFHS) <www.ffhs.org.uk>
<www.bbc.co.uk/history/familyhistory>
<www.familyrecords.gov.uk>
<www.westminster.gov.uk/communityandliving/registrar/familytree/s>
<www.ancestry.co.uk>

Information about genealogy and family therapy may also be found at:

<http://genealogy.tomrue.net/html/systems.htm>

The genogram

A genogram, often used in family therapy, is like an extended family tree, but one that identifies patterns in family relationships and behaviour that might be hereditary or learned; it might also be used to map out a family medical history. Martha, for example, saw her present difficulties with her daughter reflected in her own relationship with her mother at the same age. Genograms are usually done with the help of a therapist, but if you want to make your own, bear in mind the following:

- Include at least three generations.
- Any miscarriages, terminations of pregnancy, stillbirths or other early deaths must be included.
- Include significant issues or events – major house moves, career changes, changes of faith, divorce or separation, illness, depression, hospitalization.
- Always include date, age and causes of deaths.
- Pay particular attention to illnesses in the under 50–55 age group if you are focusing on health.
- Health reports, like all family stories, shouldn't be taken at face value. Do get any health concerns checked by a doctor.
- If you need to approach family members for more information, tread carefully. Making a genogram can raise some sensitive issues, especially when entering habits such as alcoholism, drug

addiction or abusive relationships. If you do approach other people for information, be prepared for conflicting stories.

- Be careful to whom you show your genogram. It may not be a good idea to whip it out at the annual family Christmas get-together!
- You can build your genogram on a large sheet of paper (you may need three or four A4 sheets tacked together), on your computer, or online, for example at Ancestry.com.

<http://landing.ancestry.com/fhw/merc/wiz>

Other ways to build family identity

Preserving family stories

Anita

When Anita's grandmother died, her stories died with her, as well as the minutiae of life that makes up a family, such as the recipe for her famous scones, and how she used to gather damsons every summer for making jam. Like many others, Anita had meant to write them down, but had never got round to it. To Anita, it was as if a chunk of history – nearly a century – fell into the sea.

Ask older family members to write stories down themselves, or to record or dictate them. Some may prefer to create scrapbooks or memory books with you or with their grandchildren, perhaps including a simple family tree. Ask to help sort through memorabilia – an old wedding dress or baby clothes, newspaper cuttings, medals and trophies all have a story. There are online resources to help, too, such as the family story generator, which has a list of questions designed to help you create a family story to pass on to your grandchild:

<www.ourgrandchild.com/familystory/index.htm>

Ethical wills

An ethical will can be seen as a more formal variation on this. Whereas a traditional will transmits material goods, an ethical will, which has been used in Jewish history for centuries, aims to transmit your less tangible 'assets' such as your story, your values, and the lessons life has taught you. In family business, it can be used to pass the values, history and ethos of the business down to future generations. There are a growing number of legacy advisers who can help people to write an ethical will, though this depends very much on the individual's personality. Some prefer to do it alone. Privacy and the freedom to express oneself without constraints or an audience can be very important aspects of an ethical will for people.

Re-writing your family history

Another exercise that can be therapeutic, and can help you set goals for your own life, is to re-invent your family life. Write a story or create a genogram of the family you would have *liked* to have had.

Clare

Clare grew up with very controlling parents who had the doors firmly shut against the outside world. Resolutely antisocial, they had no friends and didn't really like Clare bringing anyone to the house. Clare's ideal family was a messy, sprawly large family, ever ready to hand out pizza and chips to all comers. She envisaged her ideal as being untidy and disorganized, but friendly and welcoming.

Family websites

A family website is a fun project and a way of sharing with family members who may live far away. It can be a forum for celebrating birthdays and Christmas, or simple events like the weekend picnic noted to be so sadly in decline by Professor Putnam. It's somewhere to post family photos and drawings by children (and adults). You should, of course, bear basic web safety in mind, such as not sharing your surname, address, location or school address. For more ideas, visit:

<http://familyinternet.about.com/b/a/187746.htm>
<www.myfamily.com>

Family mottoes

Ben Jonson teased his fellow playwright Will Shakespeare about the trouble the latter took to obtain a family coat-of-arms, which was a golden yellow spear, the colour of which Ben Jonson mocked in his play *Every Man out of his Humour*: 'Let the word be not without mustard. Your crest is very rare, sir.' Shakespeare's motto was 'Not without right' (*Non sanz droict*).

Family mottoes are well worth examining, even lightheartedly. They often encapsulate family myths and values, sometimes ironically: 'No secrets in this house'; 'This is Freedom Hall'. Some people might be tempted to define their family mottoes even more brutally: Cheryl, for example, gave 'Money at all costs' as her family motto, while Keith replied, even more simply, 'Me first'.

More seriously, mottoes might be implicit or explicit in the family code of behaviour, and are often directly motivational, such as 'Never give up' or 'Work before everything else'. Or they may define a philosophy, 'Moderation in all things' or 'This too shall pass'. Maybe now is the time to write your own family motto!

12

Lifestyle and stress management

Small everyday adjustments can make a surprising difference to how well you manage both family and stress.

Family diet

Meals can be 'loaded' when it comes to family. You're often serving more than just food – memories and attitudes mingle with the hors d'oeuvres, and the food is to be approved as well as eaten.

Family meals can, however, be a time for relaxing together, strengthening family ties and keeping up with the latest family news. Meals with the immediate family are well documented to be good for health. A survey by the University of Minnesota showed that frequent family meals are related to better nutritional intake, and a lower risk for eating disorders and substance abuse. A Harvard study showed that eating family dinners together most or all days of the week was associated with eating more healthily, with families generally consuming higher amounts of important nutrients such as calcium, fibre, iron, Vitamins B6 and B12, C and E. Eating together is also associated with higher academic performance in children.

Here are some tips:

- Try to create a relaxed atmosphere at family meals. Don't get stressed out trying to make everything perfect. Ask family members to help instead.
- Keep meals simple. You do not have to reproduce the elaborate home-cooked meals of your childhood – though the traditional roast is actually one of the simplest meals to prepare as it cooks by itself in the oven with minimal attention.
- Cook for the freezer at weekends – food such as soups and casseroles – so you always have a nutritious option available.
- Take advantage of ready-cooked meals, such as a freshly roasted chicken from the supermarket, served with baked potatoes and salad.

Anti-stress diet

The stress hormone cortisol is an appetite trigger – its purpose is to help you refuel for the next 'emergency'. This is one reason why, under stress, we may put on weight. The more stressed you are, the more cortisol you produce, and the more you eat – usually carbohydrates which have a tendency to cling to the waistline, creating the risk of heart disease and diabetes.

Beat the 'CortiZone'

Dr Pamela Peeke, professor of medicine at the University of Maryland, and an expert on the effects of stress on body weight, suggests ways to beat the effect of cortisol:

- Eat a healthy breakfast, no later than 9 a.m., such as low-fat yogurt, fruit, wholegrain cereal or toast; or oatmeal with raisins and skimmed milk; or a boiled egg.
- Eat a small snack approximately three hours after breakfast. Suggestions: fruit, low-fat yogurt, low-fat cottage cheese, or another type of low-fat cheese.
- Try to eat lunch no later than 1.30 p.m., with a healthy balance of high-quality, low-stress protein, fat and carbohydrates.
- Three hours after lunch is usually the beginning of the 'CortiZone', when stress hormones plummet along with energy and mental concentration. It's also the most popular time for stress-related eating, when you grab a chocolate bar or piece of cake for a quick energy boost. Instead, eat something that provides high-quality, low-stress energy. Combinations of protein and carbohydrates are ideal, such as low-fat or fat-free yogurt or cottage cheese, along with a piece of fruit.
- Dinner should be from 6 p.m. to 7.30 p.m. It should include soup or salad, vegetables and a source of protein, such as poultry, lean red meat, fish, legumes or a veggie burger, and fruit for dessert.

Other tips for eating to beat stress

Eating to beat stress is really about eating a healthy balanced diet by making wise food choices, according to the European Food Information Council (EUFIC).

We should all know the basics of healthy eating by now – more fresh food, fewer processed and convenience foods, less sugar and salt, less alcohol, and so on. In particular, EUFIC makes the following points with regard to stress and nutrition:

Vitamin C

The body produces adrenaline when under stress, a process that requires Vitamin C. Long-term stress can raise the need for Vitamin C, and as the human body does not produce Vitamin C itself, we need to obtain it from Vitamin C-rich foods such as oranges, kiwi fruit, berries, peppers, potatoes and broccoli.

Beta-carotene

If you are undergoing long-term stress, EUFIC also recommends plenty of foods rich in beta-carotene (a precursor of Vitamin A) to help boost the immune system, such as carrots, deep-green leafy vegetables and yellow and orange fruits.

Folic acid

This is also vital for a strong immune system and specifically helps to defend the body against infections. Folic acid is found in black-eyed beans, spinach and other green leafy vegetables.

Zinc

This also helps the immune system and good sources of zinc include crabmeat, oysters, wheatgerm, liver, pumpkin seeds and red meat.

Protein

The body's need for protein can also increase when under permanent stress, to help boost the immune system. Try to have some kind of fish, chicken, turkey, lean red meat, eggs, milk or beans at meals. Oily fish like salmon, trout, tuna and sardines are good choices because they also supply essential fats capable of thinning the blood, and so may help to counteract the blood-thickening properties of adrenaline.

Magnesium

Professor Strepp Porta, professor of endocrinology at the University of Graz, has found that the need for magnesium increases greatly in today's type of prolonged stress. Magnesium is available from green vegetables such as spinach, legumes, nuts and seeds, and whole, unrefined grains. Some comes from tap water but this varies – hard water contains more magnesium than does soft water.

Water – make sure you drink enough

Low levels of dehydration – just 10 per cent – are a common cause of tiredness, headaches, or lack of concentration. Losing 2 per cent of body weight as water causes a 20 per cent drop in energy levels. If you are feeling stressed and lacking in energy, it's worth checking your water intake.

Not enough water can lead to problems with kidneys, mental functioning, your digestive system and heart. The amount of blood in your body reflects the amount of water you drink. If your fluid intake goes down, so too does your volume of blood, so that less is available for the heart, brain, muscles and all the important organs. The less blood delivered to these crucial organs, the less oxygen they receive, and the less able they are to perform their normal tasks.

Stress, alcohol and caffeine all influence the amount of water and the speed that your body loses it. An average amount of water loss per day is two cups through breathing, two cups through invisible perspiration, and six cups through urination and bowel movements. That is a total of ten cups lost per day without taking into account perspiration from exercise or hard work, excessively dry air, or alcohol and caffeine consumption.

Thirst itself is not a reliable sign of dehydration – one symptom of dehydration can be hunger, leading people to eat rather than drink. Usually, by the time you feel thirsty, you are already slightly dehydrated. The key is to keep up a regular intake of fluid during the day, aiming to have around six to eight glasses a day. Have a glass of water around; mix it with a little fruit juice; enjoy herbal teas. Take a bottle of water when you go out. Offer family members a nice glass of sparkling water rather than the gin and tonic or wine that's guaranteed to fuel old arguments!

Caffeine

Like other drinks containing caffeine, including tea and soft drinks, coffee is a stress drink. Caffeine stimulates the production of the stress hormones cortisol and adrenaline, and also blocks adenosine, a brain chemical that calms the body. One study at Duke University showed that people who had two or three cups of coffee during four hours had an adrenaline level 37 per cent higher than those who didn't drink coffee.

Caffeine gets into your system within minutes, peaks at about an hour, but stays in your system for some four to six hours, or even longer the older you get. So the caffeine has a cumulative effect, and can prevent sleep, causing even more stress. If you feel you are having too much caffeine, just have a couple of cups of coffee in the morning, and then herbal teas or water for the rest of the day.

Try to sleep more

Sleep experts estimate that more than half of our busy population is walking around in some degree of sleep deprivation, and they claim that as a society we are going short of sleep by an hour to an hour and a half a night. Biologically, we are designed to have around nine hours of sleep a night, according to sleep expert Professor Stanley Coren from the University of British Columbia in Canada, whereas many people get far less.

Symptoms of sleep deprivation include agitation, moodiness, grumpiness, irritability, waking up feeling unrefreshed, and problems with short-term memory, attention and concentration. As well as contributing to traffic accidents, greater risk of infection (because lack of sleep affects our immune system, which is stimulated during sleep), mistakes at work, impaired concentration and memory – and stress – lack of sleep even affects intelligence. Professor Coren found that one hour's lost sleep out of eight results in a drop of one IQ point, while for every additional hour lost, you drop two points.

Sleep deprivation actually produces many of the same symptoms as stress. One study found that four days' sleep deprivation resulted in the same symptoms of clinical depression too.

Are you short of sleep?

- Do you need an alarm clock to wake you up?
- Do you wake up feeling refreshed or tired?
- How tired are you during the day? Do you run out of energy mid-afternoon?
- How much sleep do you get when you don't have to get up early – for example, at weekends or on holiday?
- How soon do you fall asleep at night? 'Sleep latency' is the criterion used by sleep researchers to measure how sleep-deprived you are. Around 15–20 minutes is considered normal; less indicates sleep deprivation.

Getting more sleep

Try going to bed earlier (staying in bed later is more difficult to manage for most people). Ban the television from the bedroom, and listen to soothing music instead. Have a snack of a milky drink and a sandwich. If you're tense, try the classic remedy of a warm bath. Allow yourself to relax. With persistence, your sleep rhythms will adjust.

Breathing

We all know how to breathe. It occurs automatically, spontaneously, naturally. We are breathing even when we are not thinking about it. Yet we can develop unhealthy habits without being aware of it. We may assume a slouched posture that diminishes lung capacity and then take shortened breaths. Under stress, we may take faster and more shallow breaths without noticing – sometimes the prelude to feeling light-headed or experiencing a full-blown panic attack.

Yogis realized the vital importance of an adequate oxygen supply thousands of years ago. They developed and perfected various breathing techniques. These breathing exercises are particularly important for people who have sedentary jobs and spend most of the day in offices. Typically, a sedentary person, when confronted with a perplexing problem, tends to lean forward, draw his arms together, and bend his head down, resulting in reduced lung capacity. The muscles in the arms, neck and chest contract. The muscles that move the thorax and control inhalation and muscular tenseness clamp down and restrict the exhalation. The breaths become shorter and shorter. It's a tiring posture, because of the decreased circulation of the blood and the decreased availability of oxygen for the blood.

Modern technology reduces our need for physical activity, and so there is less need to breathe deeply, and we develop the shallow breathing habit. Stress can also makes us breathe more quickly and less deeply.

Deep breathing exercise to combat stress

- Sit or stand, making sure you are relaxed and that your posture is good so that your lungs have enough room to expand.
- Breathe through your nose.
- Inhale, filling first the lower part of your lungs, then the middle part, and finally the upper part.
- Hold your breath for a few seconds.
- Exhale slowly. Relax your abdomen and chest.

That's all there is to it!

The Relaxation Response – a longer breathing exercise

The Relaxation Response is the name of a book published by Dr Herbert Benson of Harvard University (Avon Books, New York 1975). In a series of experiments, Dr Benson established that meditation and relaxation techniques had a real effect on reducing stress, resulting in deep relaxation, slowed heartbeat and breathing, and reduced oxygen consumption:

- Sit quietly and comfortably.
- Close your eyes.
- Start by relaxing the muscles of your feet and then work your way up your body, relaxing the various muscles.
- Focus your attention on your breathing.
- Breathe in deeply and then let your breath out. Count your breaths, and say the number of the breath as you let it out (this gives you something to do with your mind, helping you to avoid distraction).
- Do this for 10–20 minutes.

Keep checking

One of the most important anti-stress measures you can adopt is to attempt to keep a check on yourself. Try making the simple decision to check yourself out perhaps three times each day. This would take the form of, say, a momentary pause. It could be an early morning reflection as you think of the coming day; a pause in your routine at work; a slowing down for a moment as you hurry along a crowded pavement, and questioning such hurry and the stress it might bring. In this way, you're less likely to react automatically to the annoying letter or e-mail, the irritating phone call, the unsatisfying family interaction.

Gary

Gary had suffered from migraine-related double vision for ten years. 'Stress', his doctors had diagnosed. Gary changed his life via making daily checks on his stress level. Am I breathing properly? Are my shoulders bunched up? Am I clenching my fists? Am I eating too quickly? (Stop hurrying!) So great is the change in Gary's life from these simple procedures that, though agnostic, he feels he has visited Lourdes.

Stress is cumulative, even on a daily basis; it can build up between breakfast and lunchtime, and then again up until bedtime. So if we can discipline ourselves to have this series of pauses, it can help us to evaluate our stress levels.

Relaxation techniques

Relaxation techniques usually involve refocusing your attention to something calming and increasing awareness of your body – the latter is especially important in stress where you may not be aware of your scrunched-up shoulders, clenched hands and shallow breathing. It doesn't matter which technique you choose. What *does* matter is that you try to practise relaxation regularly.

There are several main types of relaxation techniques, including:

Autogenic Training (AT)

In AT, you use both visual imagery and body awareness to reduce stress. Typically, you repeat words or suggestions in your mind to help you relax and reduce muscle tension. You may imagine a peaceful place and then focus on controlled, relaxing breathing, slowing your heart rate, or focus on different physical sensations, such as relaxing each arm or leg separately.

Progressive muscle relaxation

This technique focuses on slowly tensing and then relaxing each muscle group so that you become more aware of the difference between muscle tension and relaxation. You may choose to start by tensing and relaxing the muscles in your toes and progressively working your way up to your neck and head. Tense your muscles for at least five seconds, relax for 30 seconds, then repeat.

Visualization

We all have a natural tendency to daydream; this technique focuses this. It involves forming mental images to take a visual journey to a peaceful, calming place or situation. Try to use as many senses as you can, including smells, sights, sounds and textures. If you imagine relaxing by the sea, for example, think about the warmth of the sun, the sound of crashing waves, the feel of the grains of sand and the smell of salt water. This works especially well if you use it in combination with a relaxation technique, or just sit in a comfortable position, eyes closed, allowing yourself a few minutes of time out.

You can also use visualization to imagine yourself achieving goals such as becoming healthier and more relaxed, doing well in personal interactions, and handling conflict in better ways.

Meditation

This can help combat stress and revitalize the mind. First choose a word or phrase – such as 'peace' or 'one'. Then sit in a comfortable position, close your eyes, relax your muscles, and allow yourself to breathe slowly and naturally. As you exhale, repeat the word or phrase. After doing this for 10–20 minutes once or twice a day, you may notice your stress drifting away, along with your exhalations.

The benefits of lying down

Lying down increases the blood flow to the brain, bringing more oxygen and so more energy, and generally making the whole brain more effective in how it works.

The brain's right hemisphere recognizes patterns and symbols, and processes them instantly. The left hemisphere is responsible for more linear activities: logical thought, analysis and reading. In industrialized societies the right hemisphere predominates. Also, when people are fatigued, the right hemisphere predominates. Think about how you process information when you're really tired. It becomes almost impossible to read, but visual stimulation can take on added intensity. Also, when people are cognitively overloaded, as happens a great deal in our fast-paced, technology-dominated society, the brain starts screening out information. Time to lie down! Lying down lets the blood flow to the head, and generally relaxes and refreshes you.

Yoga

This is one of the oldest and most effective forms of stress management there is. Many of today's popular techniques found to reduce stress have their roots in yoga, such as controlled breathing, meditation, physical movement, mental imagery and stretching. Yoga:

- reduces stress, anxiety and muscle tension;
- promotes sound sleep;
- relieves allergy and asthma symptoms;
- lowers blood pressure and heart rate;
- helps with giving up smoking;
- increases strength and flexibility;
- slows the ageing process.

Laughter yoga

But if you want yoga with a little twist, you might find laughter yoga interesting. Dr Madan Kataria, in Bombay, started laughter clubs featuring yoga in 1995 after reading about the medical benefits of laughter. Studies have demonstrated – as if we didn't already know it – that when we laugh, our bodies release hormones and chemicals that have positive effects on our systems. Stress is reduced, blood pressure drops, depression is lifted, your immune system is boosted, and more. Humour is a recommended coping strategy for stress.

There are now nearly two thousand laughter yoga clubs in India, and an additional 700 around the world. The idea is to combine yoga stretches with laughter and, according to Dr Kataria, it doesn't matter if it's just pretend laughter as your body doesn't know the difference. Specific techniques include:

- A 'ho, ho, ha-ha-ha' chant.
- The 'lion laugh', a variation on the lion pose that involves thrusting the tongue right out of the mouth to refresh the face muscles.

Effectiveness of knitting relaxation

Researchers at Harvard Medical School made the ultimate anti-stress discovery – that knitting, crocheting and embroidery are as effective as meditation, yoga or chanting in triggering the body's relaxation response. In knitting, the repetitive motions block the stress hormone noradrenaline, which in turn lowers blood pressure and your heart rate, leaving you feeling more peaceful. In one study, needleworkers' heart rates dropped by 11 beats a minute while they worked. They also ended up with a nice pair of mittens!

Stress and lack of natural light

Our 'car culture', technology and methods of working ensure that today we receive less natural light than ever before. The last two or three generations are the first to be spending at least three-quarters of their time in artificial light. Many of us live, work and travel shut out from natural light. Our changed exposure to light is believed to account for the increase in seasonal affective disorder (SAD), which affects an estimated one in twenty people and leads to symptoms of depression, lethargy and decreased ability to deal with stress. Remember the classic Christmas family squabble? Could it be that SAD sheds new light on why we find certain relatives so difficult? Some people have found that they develop SAD after a stressful event such as a bereavement or other family crisis in winter. If you do feel you are suffering from SAD, or any type of depression, do consult your doctor.

(See *Coping with Seasonal Affective Disorder* by Fiona Marshall and Peter Cheevers (Sheldon Press 2002).)

Exercise

Exercise is one of the simplest and most immediate means of tackling stress. There is abundant evidence that it works by releasing endorphins, natural chemicals that raise mood, into the body. The main problem with exercise is that you are either preaching to the converted or the uninterested. If you're one of the latter, a simple way to get more exercise into your life is to leave the car at home for two weeks. Equip yourself with a pair of comfortable walking shoes and a lightweight shopping trolley. It's an interesting exercise! Indeed, the slower pace of life, engendered by walking and public transport, can in itself lower stress levels simply by forcing you to slow down.

Keep a stress journal

For one week, note which events and situations cause a negative physical, mental or emotional response:

- Record the day and time.
- Give a brief description of the situation.
- Where were you?
- Who was involved?
- What seemed to cause the stress?
- Describe your reaction in terms of physical symptoms and feelings.
- What did you say or do?
- Finally, on a scale of 1 (not very intense) to 5 (very intense), rate the intensity of your stress.

Pets

Unlike people, and family in particular, with whom our interactions may be complex and unpredictable, pets provide a steady source of comfort, non-judgmental love and loyalty. Having something to care for may also stimulate our survival instinct – it seems many people with cancer may have lived longer because they felt that their pets needed them.

There is a great deal of evidence that pets can be good for health. A study from the State University of New York at Buffalo of stockbrokers with high blood pressure found that those given a pet had significantly lower blood pressure after six months than those without pets. One of the study's conclusions was that pet ownership is especially good for you if you have a limited support system – which sadly may be all too applicable if you are facing difficulties with your family.

Another study at the same university actually proved that pets can be more supportive in times of stress than friends or partners. The study involved 240 married couples, half of whom owned a cat or dog. Couples without pets had higher blood pressure and heart rates, a strong sign that they were feeling more stress than the pet owners. The researchers noted that judgement and criticism from others is a major source of stress.

Owning a dog may also help to ward off stress-related illness. Urban dog owners generally walk almost twice as much as their neighbours who don't have dogs, according to a study by the University of Missouri. Regular walks mean exercise, a chance to chat with people and, often, weight loss as well. People in one study who borrowed a dog and walked it for 20 minutes a day for 50 weeks, for example, lost an average of 14 pounds – more than many people lose on popular diet plans. Yet another study found that dog owners required much less medical care for stress-induced aches and pains than non-dog owners.

Research has also shown that heart attack victims who have pets live longer. Even watching a tank full of tropical fish may lower blood pressure, at least temporarily.

It doesn't matter what type of pet you choose, though it should fit your temperament, living space and lifestyle – otherwise it will only be an additional source of stress!

Music therapy

There is a growing body of evidence that music helps to alleviate stress – for example, in patients waiting to undergo surgery.

Many experts suggest that it is the rhythm of the music that helps, especially if it mimics that of the human heartbeat. Among the first stress-fighting changes that take place when we hear a tune is an increase in deep breathing. The body's production of serotonin also increases.

Playing music, no matter how badly, is also therapeutic. (I confess to strumming the Beatles' 'Hey Jude' when everyone is out!) Singing therapy is also growing in popularity. Doctors believe it encourages better posture and deeper breathing, while helping to release the body's endorphins.

Playing music in the background while we are working, unaware of the music itself, has been found to reduce stress:

- Choose music with a slow rhythm – slower than the natural heartbeat, which is about 72 beats per minute. Music that has a repeating or cyclical pattern is found to be effective in most people.
- Focus on your breathing, letting it deepen, slow down and become regular.
- Concentrate on the silence between the notes in the music; this keeps you from analysing the music and makes for better relaxation.

- When you're really stressed, choose music you are familiar with – such as a favourite oldie. Familiarity often breeds calmness.
- Go for a walk with your favourite music playing on a personal CD or MP3 player. Inhale and exhale in time with the music. Combining exercise (brisk walk), imagery and music is a great stress-reliever.
- Contact the British Society for Music Therapy: <www.bsmt.org>.

Challenge yourself

Scientists from Northwestern University in Illinois, in the USA, have studied *C. elegans*, a transparent roundworm whose biochemical environment is similar to that of humans. The scientists found that stress 'turns on' key genes which encode protective molecules, increasing the worms' lifespan. Increased temperatures, oxygen stress, bacterial and viral infections, and exposure to toxins such as heavy metals, were all found to increase stress on cells.

The research concluded that, while sustained or severe stress is definitely not good for you, it appears that an occasional burst of stress or low levels of stress can be very protective. We do need a certain amount of stress it seems.

Time management

One of the problems with stressful family situations is that they often steal more time than perhaps they merit, and certainly more time than is comfortable. Be ruthless – don't let them take over your life. By keeping a schedule, learning to say no to excessive demands on your time, and using shortcuts, you'll be less frantic, and have more time to do the things that energize and de-stress you.

While managing your time is a practical and effective way of dealing with stress, it can be one of the most difficult things to implement:

- Don't spend too much time chewing over the latest family crisis with your partner or friends. Do get it off your chest, and discuss what's bothering you, but try not to go over and over the same ground.
- Make a decision to limit time spent with troublesome family members, especially if you feel it doesn't help either them or yourself. Decide on how often you want to see members of your family – once a month? Once a year? Never?
- Set conditions and stick to them; for example, 'I will arrange to visit my brother only if we make a date and stick to it, rather than

allowing him to cancel at the last moment if he feels something better has come up.'

- Learn to say no. There are many polite ways to make it clear you don't want to get involved in family commitments or get-togethers; for example, 'I need to rest more at the moment', 'I have too much work to do', 'I'll think about whether I can manage it and let you know', 'I'm sorry, I'm not free that day'. Or you can suggest alternatives: 'I can't do it tomorrow, but maybe next week'. Perhaps set a time limit: 'I can't come for the day, but I can manage two hours in the afternoon'.

Other suggestions for dealing with stress

- *Organize.* Disorganization creates stress so take control of your time. Being more organized boosts a sense of control, which in turn reduces stress.
- *Make decisions.* Indecision increases stress. Even if you decide to do nothing and to put the question on hold – for example, with regard to moving house – it is still a decision, and so eases the stress of uncertainty.
- *Keep your living space organized.* Pay attention to your space as well as to your time. A cluttered environment can drain your energy and cause additional stress. De-clutter your home, become organized about cleaning, find a place for everything, and get rid of what you can't find a place for.
- *Leave time for the unexpected.* Don't over-fill your time with commitments. A stressful situation needs time, both to take in what the situation entails, and how to deal with it. Leave room in your life so you have time enough to respond organically, rather than making an instant 'knee-jerk' reaction.
- *Choose friends carefully.* Your choice of friends can be key to stress management. Friends should be people who help us to increase our strengths and create creative solutions to stressful situations.
- *Stop and look at yourself.* Take time to recognize your own signals of stress such as irritability, short fuse, poor sleep, or over-working. By becoming more conscious of stress factors in our lives, we avoid becoming the victim of the 'it just sneaked up on me' syndrome. As you become aware of these signs, you can begin to take action in advance; that is, to be proactive rather than reactive.
- *Seek out resources.* Depending on personal taste and budget, there are a myriad of resources to help you relax, unwind and get away

from your stressful family! T'ai chi, reflexology, homeopathy, herbal medicine and massage therapy are just some of the solutions people seek out. Or it could be allowing yourself time for a hobby you've always wanted to pursue such as horse riding, rug making, tennis or travel. Rather than letting family members mop up your time, use it the way you want to.

- *Accept what cannot be changed.* Take on board the fact that you can't control everything or make everyone happy, least of all the disruptive, dysfunctional and unpleasant adults in your wider family. Take control of what you can control – your working hours, your health, your time. Ensure you have enough breaks, and accept that it's OK to make mistakes.

Conclusion

With regard to the question as to whether Earth has ever been visited by extra-terrestrials, I go along with Stephen Hawkins, who feels that we would have 'known' if we had been visited by beings from outer space for he feels the encounter would have been 'uncomfortable'. After all, it's bad enough when family descend on us from on high. We know all too well when we have been visited by the difficult relatives of this book – the encounter is, indeed, 'uncomfortable'.

In dealing with family stress, it's hard to take drastic action to eliminate the problem overnight. It's not like giving up smoking or drinking. Family tend to stick around. Of course, you can move far, far away, a solution that many have found effective. George Burns once joked that happiness is having a loving family, but best if they are in another city. Or you could decide not to see your family any more. This works best if there are no unresolved issues, otherwise family members tend to live on, alive and well, in your head.

Meanwhile I hope this book has helped to tackle any problems you may face with your difficult family. That the family itself is under stress today is really nothing new. Families have always been diverse and fragile; and I go along with Stephanie Coontz, who feels that our expectations of today's family are unrealistic, and based on nostalgia for a largely mythical past of 'traditional values' that prevents us from getting on with real family life.

It's a myth that has a huge grip on our collective imagination. Professor Stephen Jay Gould's analysis (*Bully for Brontosaurs*, Penguin 1991) of the Cardiff Giant hoax in 1869 – a crude stone carving fabricated by a rogue and passed off as a petrified fossil of great antiquity on palpably flimsy grounds – demonstrates how we ignore the evidence in our quest for our origins. We need to believe things about our race or family even in the face of the evidence.

I started this book with a story about chimps. To put things in perspective, it's not all so benign in the animal world as the chimp family dynamic would lead us to expect. Compared with humans, as Edward Osborne Wilson points out, some species of monkeys, Madras baboons and langur monkeys in particular, are so aggressive that, were they given nuclear weapons (and the cognitive and muscular ability to work them), we would all be wiped off the planet in 30 minutes – which surely makes the possibilities for our own family relationships look not so bad after all, doesn't it?

Useful addresses

UK

Association for Family Therapy (AFT)
7 Executive Suite
St James Court
Wilderspool Causeway
Warrington
Cheshire WA4 6PS
Tel.: 01925 444414
Website: www.aft.org.uk

Association of Family Business Advisers
University of Gloucestershire
The Park
Cheltenham GL50 2RH
Tel.: 01242 714700
Website: www.glos.ac.uk/faculties/ugbs/info/family/afba.cfm

British Association for Behavioural and Cognitive Psychotherapies (BABCP)
Victoria Buildings
9–13 Silver Street
Bury BL9 0EU
Tel.: 0161 797 4484
Website: www.babcp.org.uk
Email: babcp@babcp.com

British Association for Counselling and Psychotherapy (BACP)
BACP House
15 St John's Business Park
Lutterworth
Leics LE17 4HP
Tel.: 0870 443 5252
Website: www.bacp.co.uk

Carers UK
20–25 Glasshouse Yard
London EC1A 4JS
Tel.: 020 7490 8818
CarersLine: 0808 808 7777 (Wednesday and Thursday, 10 a.m. to 12 noon/2p.m. to 4 p.m.)
Website: www.carersuk.org

Depression Alliance
212 Spitfire Studios
63–71 Collier Street
London N1 9BE
Tel.: 0845 123 23 20
Website: www.depressionalliance.org

International Stress Management Association
PO Box 26
South Petherton TA13 5WY
Tel: 07000 780430
Website: www.isma.org.uk

Mental Health Foundation
London Office
Ninth Floor, Sea Containers House
20 Upper Ground
London SE1 9QB
Tel.: 020 7803 1100
Website: www.mentalhealth.org.uk
Email: mhf@mhf.org.uk

MIND/National Association for Mental Health
Granta House
15–19 Broadway
London E15 4BQ
Tel.: 020 8519 2122
MindinfoLine: 0845 766 0163 (9.15 a.m. to 5.15 p.m., Monday to Friday)
Website: www.mind.org.uk

Princess Royal Trust for Carers
142 Minories
London EC3N 1LB
Tel.: 020 7480 7788
Website: www.carers.org

Relate
Herbert Gray College
Little Church Street
Rugby
Warwickshire CV21 3AP
Tel.: 0845 456 1310
Website: www.relate.org.uk

SAD Association
PO Box 989
Steyning BN44 3HG
Website: www.sada.org.uk

Samaritans
The Upper Mill
Kingston Road
Ewell
Surrey KT17 2AF
Tel.: 020 8394 8300
Helpline (24 hours): 08457 90 90 90
Website: www.samaritans.org.uk

Scottish Family Business Association
Unit 12
Barncluith Business Centre
Townhead Street
Hamilton ML3 7DP
Tel.: 01698 427 653
Website: www.sfba.co.uk

USA

The Academy of Cognitive Therapy
One Belmont Avenue, Suite 700
Bala Cynwyd
PA 19004-1610
Tel.: (610) 664-1273
Website: www.academyofct.org

American Society of Clinical Psychopharmacology
PO Box 40395
Glen Oaks
NY 11004
Tel.: 718 470 4007
Website: www.ascpp.org

Depression Awareness, Recognition and Treatment (DART)
National Institute of Mental Health
5600 Fishers Lane
Rockville
MD 20857
Tel.: (800) 421 4211
Website: www.nimh.nih.gov/healthinformation/depressionmenu.cfm

Depression and Related Affected Disorders Association (DRADA)
Meyer 4–181
600 North Wolfe Street
Baltimore
MD 21205
Tel.: (301) 955 4647

National Association for Seasonal Affective Disorder (NOSAD)
PO Box 40190
Washington
DC 20016

Further reading

Boss, Pauline, *Family Stress: Classic and Contemporary Readings*. Sage Publications, California, 2002.

Byng-Hall, John, *Rewriting Family Scripts: Improvisation and Systems Change*. Guilford Press, New York, 1998.

Campbell Slan, Joanna, *Scrapbook Storytelling: Saving Family Stories and Memories with Photos, Journalling and Your Own Creativity*. EFG Publishing, St Louis, Missouri, 2002.

Coontz, Stephanie, *The Way We Never Were: American Families and the Nostalgia Trap*. Basic Books, New York, 2000.

Featherstone, Katie et al., *Risky Relations: Family, Kinship, and the New Genetics*. Berg Publishers, Oxford, 2006.

Felder, Dr Leonard, *When Difficult Relatives Happen to Good People*. Rodale Books, Emmaus, Pennsylvania, 2003.

Gillis, John R., *A World of Their Own Making: Myth, Ritual, and the Quest for Family Values*. Harvard University Press, Cambridge, Massachusetts, 1997.

McCall, Bridget, *The Complete Carer's Guide*. Sheldon Press, London, 2007.

McCubbin, Hamilton et al., *Stress, Coping, and Health in Families: Sense of Coherence and Resiliency*. Sage Publications, California, 2003.

McGoldrick, Monica et al., *Genograms: Assessment and Intervention*, W.W. Norton & Co., New York, 1999.

McKenry, Patrick C. and Price, Sharon J., *Families and Change: Coping with Stressful Events and Transitions*. Sage Publications, California, 2005.

Putnam, Robert, *Bowling Alone: The Collapse and Revival of American Community*, Simon & Schuster, New York, 2001.

Robinson, Jo and Coppock Staeheli, Jean, *Unplug the Christmas Machine: A Complete Guide to Putting Love and Joy Back into the Season*. William Morrow, New York, 1991.

Stinnett, Nick et al., *Fantastic Families: 6 Proven Steps to Building a Strong Family*. Howard Books, New York, 1999.

Stone, Elizabeth, *Black Sheep and Kissing Cousins: How our Family Stories Shape Us*. Transaction Publishers, New Jersey, 2004.

Index